ABOVE the FRAY

"I have coached, trained, inspired, and learned from hundreds of business owners and employees all over the world, and one thing I know for certain is that a company will succeed during good times and bad only when it operates from a strong foundation of core values, principles, and philosophies. Unfortunately this is rarely addressed by business leaders until the going gets tough—when it is often too late. In *Above The Fray*, Larry Parman comprehensively guides you step-by-step through the process of building your company from the inside-out, ensuring you and your business thrive when others suffer. Whether just beginning or highly experienced, smart and savvy business leaders should carefully study and act upon this book today."

— **Lee Milteer**, Best-Selling Author; International Performance and Productivity Coach; Award-Winning Professional Speaker; TV Personality. www.leemilteer.com

"Life's journey seems to always be the best teacher. Larry Parman's crafty use of real-life experiences creates a refreshing approach to management and leadership with *Above the Fray*. Great lessons for newcomers and veterans of business."

— **Mark Walker**, Former President & CEO, United Way Silicon Valley

"Larry Parman has written a book designed with the business owner in mind. Each chapter reveals real life experiences of his business life in the trenches. The wisdom contained in this book is priceless."

— **Michael Bonfrisco**, Esq., The Bonfrisco Law Firm, LLC.

"Larry Parman has a very rare ability to see any situation in light of the wisdom and experience he carries, and to put his insight into words. This book is both deeply insightful and tremendously practical. I've had the opportunity to learn from Mr. Parman as a coach and mentor for several years, and will return to this book regularly to continue learning these principles and how to apply them to everyday business and life."

— **Catherine Hammond**, Esq., Hammond Law Group

"The beauty of Larry Parman's *Above the Fray* is that it puts at the reader's fingertips transformational knowledge derived from his own personal life experiences, as well as the knowledge and life experiences shared with him by others who long ago learned the secret that a successful business requires more than technical knowledge and expertise. Rather, to have a successful business, the CEO or business owner must work on the business, above the fray of the day-to-day details of service or product delivery. The CEO must also have the courage of his or her convictions, and an intense present focus on the future they seek to achieve. The courage to move forward in uncertain or turbulent times, where others fear to go, because they recognize that uncertain and turbulent times offer great opportunities. Therefore, if what you seek is a better, more balanced life, derived from an enlightened way to transform your life's work into a more successful endeavor that enriches the lives of others, then you should read and heed Larry Parman's pearls of wisdom contained in *Above the Fray*."

— **Stephen A. Mendel**, The Mendel Law Firm, LP

"An insightful work, long needed in a single volume, from an enormously well qualified spokesman for more effective business management and leadership. Since Larry Parman has seen it all, in good times and bad, we can all benefit from his experience."

— **Brad Swickey**, President & CEO, Valliance Bank

"Larry Parman is a deep thinker for whom I have a great deal of admiration—over the years, his advice to me has been invaluable. In this book, he demonstrates practical, concrete actions which will help guide you to successful outcomes in business, but not before explicitly identifying the deeply rooted intellectual super-structure from which he views the business world. The end result? Clarity and conviction in the face of adversity. I wish I would have read this book 10 years ago, and I know I will still be reading it many years from now."

— **John Woods**, President, Advanced Network Design, Inc.

ABOVE
the FRAY

Leading Yourself,
Your Business and
Others During
Turbulent Times

LARRY PARMAN

Glazer-Kennedy
publishing

NEW YORK

ABOVE the FRAY
Leading Yourself, Your Business and Others During Turbulent Times

© 2014 LARRY PARMAN.

Published in New York, New York, by Morgan James Publishing. Morgan James and The Entrepreneurial Publisher are trademarks of Morgan James, LLC. www.MorganJamesPublishing.com

The Morgan James Speakers Group can bring authors to your live event. For more information or to book an event visit The Morgan James Speakers Group at www.TheMorganJamesSpeakersGroup.com.

FREE eBook edition for your existing eReader with purchase

PRINT NAME ABOVE

For more information, instructions, restrictions, and to register your copy, go to **www.bitlit.ca/readers/register** or use your QR Reader to scan the barcode:

ISBN 978-0-98371-254-1 paperback
ISBN 978-0-98371-255-8 eBook
Library of Congress Control Number:
2012932343

Cover Design by:
Rachel Lopez
www.r2cdesign.com

Interior Design by:
Bonnie Bushman
bonnie@caboodlegraphics.com

In an effort to support local communities, raise awareness and funds, Morgan James Publishing donates a percentage of all book sales for the life of each book to Habitat for Humanity Peninsula and Greater Williamsburg.

Get involved today, visit
www.MorganJamesBuilds.com

This book is dedicated to those who Built It,
those who are Building It and those who aspire to Build It.

TABLE OF CONTENTS

Acknowledgement   xiii

Foreword   xv

The World of Business: Then and Now   xii
   Why Write the Book?   xix

Where It All Started For Me...   xxiv

Part 1: Philosophy   1
You Asked For It, Now Take It   5

12 Tenets of Successful Business Owners   8
   Courage   9
   Adventurous   10
   Vision   11
   Knowledgeable   12
   Present Focused, Future Directed   13
   Adaptability   14
   Committed to Continuous Improvement   16
   A Yes, Now Attitude   16
   Promise Keepers   17
   Decisive   19
   Creative   19
   Authentic   20

Caution: Obstacles Ahead!   22

The Need to Be Right   23

Underestimating the Difficulty of the Task   23

Doing It the Way You've Always Done It   25

Failing to Delegate   26

Delegating the Wrong Thing   27

Micromanaging Your Team   27

Charting Your Course   29

Some Final Thoughts on the Philosophy   31

Part II: Planning   35

Don't Start a Business; Instead Find a Market   39

It's All in the Niche   41

Turning Your Ideas into a Plan of Action   44

Business Model Options   45

The Strategic Alignment Model — Part 1: Where Are We Going?   47

What is the Current Situation?   48

Creating a Vision — If it's Cloudy in the Pulpit
it's Foggy in the Pew   56

Futurecasting   57

Vision vs. Mission   59

Adding In Your Core Values   60

Identifying Critical Success Factors   62

**The Strategic Alignment Model —
Part 2: Setting Things in Motion**   65

The Heart – The Action and Alignment Plan   65

The Difference Maker – The 30-Day Action Plan   69

Aligning for Operational Excellence   71

Alignment: The Overlooked Ingredient   71

This is How We Do Things Here   76

Keeping Score   80

Creating and Presenting Your Business Plan   82

Defining Your Purpose   82

Business Plan Essentials   83

You're Armed With a Plan…Now What?   86

Some Final Thoughts on Planning   88

Part III: People 93

Hire for Attitude and Strengths — Train for Skill 97
Know What You Want 100
It All Starts With an Ad 101
Leverage Your Time 102
Do Your Research 104
Profile Your Personnel 105
Put Your Offer in Writing 106
The 100-Day Plan 107

Leading the Cats – Managing Yourself 108
Effective Execution 108
Fitness, Vitality, Energy 110
Time Management 111

Leading the Cats — Managing Others 119
Organizational Charts 120
The Many Faces of Management 121
Building Your Team 122
Goal Setting as a Management Tool 125
The Dreaded Quarterly Review 126
The Daily Meeting 128
Letting Them Go 130
The Golden Rule 132

Some Final Thoughts on Managing Others 133

Part IV: Promotion 141

The Importance of Marketing 145

Defining Your Company's Value 148
From Vision to Value 149

Identifying Your Target Audience 153
Analyze Your Product 154
Look to Your Competition 155

Your Basic Marketing Blueprint 156
Inbound vs. Outbound 157
Message-Media-Market Match 159
Mapping Your Sales Funnel 160

Filling Your Marketing Toolbox   **165**
    Online Marketing   166
    Offline Marketing   176
    Devising Your Strategy   181

Some Final Thoughts on Marketing   **192**

Part V: Performance   195

When the Plan Fails   **199**

Continuous Improvement: The Key to Prosperity   **203**

An Exclusive Offer from Larry Parman   **205**

About the Contributors   **207**
    Ed Allen   207
    Robert Armstrong, JD   208
    Mick Aslin   208
    Bob Barnard   209
    Bryan Beaver   209
    Kelly Brown, DDS   209
    Dennis M. Curtin   210
    John Dudeck   210
    Carl Edwards   210
    Sanford M. Fisch, JD   211
    Bill Glazer   211
    Michael J. Glosserman   211
    Steve Harmon   212
    Kirk Humphreys   212
    Greg Hunt   212
    Stanley F. Hupfeld   213
    Dan Kennedy   214
    Tony Lewis   214
    Avis Parman   215
    Dick Savage   215
    Dick Seybolt   215
    Linda Winlock   215

About Larry Parman   **217**

ACKNOWLEDGEMENT

This book is a compilation of lessons I am learning from building businesses and living a life.

One lesson, constantly reinforced and therefore requiring acknowledgement, is that many obstacles we encounter are self-created. Success is mostly about setting a course, committing to it, then overcoming personal foibles that trip us up and making way for new possibilities. That was certainly the case in the journey of completing this book.

Thanks to the Morgan James publishing team for their endless patience, guidance and encouragement when my schedule, and Self, seemed to slow the process down.

Next, I would like to recognize the incredible people I interviewed for the book. Each has been friend or mentor. Most have been both. A few have realized their dream, sold their business and are now conquering new worlds. The rest continue their business journey, all with excellence. Your input helped me clarify. Thanks to each of you for sharing your valuable insights with me and the readers.

A special thanks to those in the coaching programs I lead through CEO Maestro or co-lead with others. Your relentless pursuit of excellence reminds me that the goal of effective coaching is for the student to surpass the teacher. I applaud each of you for doing just that.

A special thanks to Avis for your strength, dignity, grace under pressure, perseverance and love. You are an extraordinary example, an even better mother. I love you.

This project would still be sitting on the shelf but for Scott Parman and Kate Luther. These exceptional colleagues helped drive this project to completion with their support, encouragement, cajoling, research, writing, editing and proofing. Mistakes that appear in the book remain because I failed to listen to their suggestions.

Outstanding colleagues at my family of companies must be thanked for their continued excellence at serving our clients without fail as I completed the book. Thank you for your contribution to my journey.

To my precious friends, near and far — your mark on my life is profound. I will be in your corner beyond the end.

Finally, to Darlene, my most trusted advisor, my incredible wife. Your faith in me, your support of me, your devotion to our wonderful family and your belief in us transcends a thank you. For that, and for who you are, you have my eternal gratitude and love.

Larry Parman
August 16, 2012 (43)

FOREWORD

I've made a career out of looking at things from an unconventional perspective.

I developed marketing campaigns for some of the top brands in the country—campaigns that helped turn those brands into the household names they are today — by embracing creativity and innovation over what was safe and practical.

And when financial experts were busy telling small business owners to pull back and conserve as the economy began to decline, I showed those same businesses how to launch successful marketing campaigns and grow their companies, even when they didn't have a marketing dime to spare.

Like I said, I've never been one for convention.

So, when I sat down to write this forward, it didn't take long to realize that it was the lack of convention in the book that appealed to me the most.

Above the Fray is about finding that new perspective... the one that allows you to see past the status quo and find new ways to achieve your goals. It's written for business owners and entrepreneurs, but many of the philosophies that form its foundation could be applied to all walks of life, personal or professional.

I mean, let's be honest: when was the last time that a handshake and a promise were all it took to close a deal? How long has it been since your professional agenda was in sync with your personal values? I believe it's for this very reason that we're seeing the revolution in consciousness I've talked about before and it's because of this upheaval that today's corporate world isn't the safe haven it used to be. Globalization and technology alone have completely reshaped the way we do business, from production and manufacturing, right down to our methods for interacting with consumers.

And it's not just the companies that have changed—the consumer has evolved as well. They're smarter, savvier and certainly more cautious about who they do business with, making it all the more important to build your company around a solid set of principles and practices from the get go.

And that's what this book is all about. The days of making money without regard for method or consequence are quickly falling away. Today's consumer not only wants a product they can use, but they want to buy it from a company they can trust. And building that trust requires you to have more than a business plan... as Larry Parman calls it, you need a *thrival plan*... you need vision.

And you need to see it from above the fray.

Jay Conrad Levinson
The Father of Guerrilla Marketing
Author, "Guerrilla Marketing" series of books.
Over 21 million sold; now in 63 languages

THE WORLD OF BUSINESS:
THEN AND NOW

Turbulence kills. Pilots, newspaper reports and the FAA confirm it. Less understood is that turbulence kills in the business world as well.

Above the Fray is about developing a series of systems that allow you not to just survive turbulence in the marketplace, but to thrive in the face of it. A "Turbulence-Thrival" plan, if you will.

Success in business has always been about doing a few things well. Investigate opportunity, prepare for adversity, staff for strategy based on strengths, execute and deliver, monitor and measure, review and refine and re-execute ...every day...and fast, with a sense of urgency before the premise of your plan is destroyed by...Turbulence.

There was a time when starting a new business was as easy as opening a bank account, hanging your shingle and getting the word out through a newspaper ad or good old word-of-mouth. These companies were often started on nothing more than a hope and a prayer and when they survived— *if* they survived — it was a matter of will power and perseverance. Of course, those days are long gone... and they've been replaced by incredibly turbulent times.

In the last decade, we've faced not one but two recessions, with the most recent 2008-2009 version hitting us the hardest. Unemployment remains high while wages haven't grown much at all. We've watched our financial institutions scramble to remain solvent. We've sat helpless as our retirement portfolios went up in smoke. Thank goodness for the recent Federal Reserve Bank induced stock market rebound or the word "turbulent" might not even cover the road that lied ahead.

We've faced 9/11, the housing bubble and a slew of financial scandals and scams that's left us wondering just how naïve we really are and what else we might have overlooked.

As a result, consumer confidence continues to rise and fall almost as much as the stock market, causing business owners to walk a fine line between filing bankruptcy and breaking even. And alongside the market forces of technology, competition, consumer and shareholder expectations, it appears our government has become an enemy, by design and policy.

In short, it hasn't been pretty and the damage has been severe. But we are after all, a capitalist country and if there's one thing that will survive no matter what, it's our ability to find new ways to make money. I've never seen government policy outsmart a prepared and committed entrepreneur nor has turbulence ever truly had the final word.

We might be down, but we're far from out and now that we recognize turbulence as a permanent fixture in the business world, we need to decide how to deal with it.

It was recognition of this new environment—this permanent turbulence — that inspired this book.

Because turbulence is now the new normal. And it's creating unparalleled challenges to business owners and CEOs worldwide. Of course, it can also create tremendous opportunities . . . but only if you're prepared. So, while this book does cover some business basics, it's not the technician that will reap the biggest rewards.

It's the dreamers… the risk takers… the visionaries that ask "what if."

And if that's you, you're going to need all the help you can get.

Now, I know what you're saying… you've got it all under control. And to that I reply, "sorry, but you don't." There's nothing about running a business that's "controlled"… that's a fantasy. And the sooner you wake up to this reality, the better off you'll be.

The business bookshelves are teeming with terrific books written for the technician. Topics on strategy, sales, management, organizational theory and motivation abound. What you need now is an effective way to apply those strategies and techniques to today's turbulent environment, and *Above the Fray* was written to do exactly that.

And that's an important distinction.

Because the business we do can have a tremendous effect on other people's lives. In fact, those who apply the principles and philosophies I've outlined in this book may well, at some point, have more influence on our society and culture than most of our U.S. presidents for the past one hundred years.

Think Steve Jobs, Bill Gates, Michael Dell and the two college students who masterminded Google, Larry Page and Sergey Brin. These, like the other countless entrepreneurs in countless fields, were driven by an idea and relentlessly drove it to excellence. Their impact in our daily lives is extraordinary and it is the new standard to which most entrepreneurs aspire. This book still requires you to possess the seed of the idea of course, but it will help you formulate a strategy for implementing that idea so it has the best chance for success.

WHY WRITE THE BOOK?

So, why take on such a challenging project? The reason is simple. I believe such a book is needed. If we want to recover from these fragile times, if we want to achieve success in this new and unpredictable world, then this book is long overdue.

There have been seismic shifts in the paradigms that govern how businesses must behave to be successful and being able to adjust to these shifts will be what makes or breaks your business. And what's changing isn't just the way we fund our business or hire our personnel… instead, it's how we secure and process information and make decisions about our vision, as well as how we utilize various tools and strategies to convert our vision into reality. And, the speed with which we do it.

And the traditional framework for these decisions no longer exists— we are now navigating through unchartered territory in the business world so relying on the way you've "always done it" no longer keeps you in the game.

Last week I was visiting with a colleague who suggested he could not write a book without significant research, without knowing that what he shared with readers would meet with the approval of the professed experts who might judge him.

And while I admire that commitment, pleasing the experts is not what this book is about. It's about helping you be more effective, in your professional and personal life. This book draws on real world experience—mine and others—so that you can start to prepare for what lies ahead... and hopefully lead your enterprise through those turbulent times successfully.

If you are a business owner, entrepreneur or CEO, and if those objectives appeal to you, this book will be helpful. Implementing the principles in this book means you will become a more effective leader of yourself and of others. Performance will improve . . . and so will your bottom line.

Now, since this is an "experience-based" book, I will focus on principles I learned while in the trenches, dealing with the grist of business issues. This is about my experiences, my lessons learned... but you'll find that those lessons ring true on a much grander scale. And yes, I'm still in those trenches, working as a professional on a journey of trying to get better every day and become more successful because of it.

In addition to my personal experiences, you'll also find tips and lessons learned from some very bright people who have volunteered to share their thoughts. Some are CEOs and business owners. Others come from seemingly unrelated disciplines. You may wonder what you have to learn from them, but I can assure you that one of my greatest learning treasures has been from those in unrelated fields. For some, their primary focus is not, or was not, the business world and I challenge you to open your mind and heart to the lessons of these outstanding achievers. Virtually all are still in the trenches, getting after it every day. The few who are not have recently sold their company, or retired, and are only months away from active involvement. Either way, I believe you'll find wisdom throughout their comments.

This isn't to say that there's not still much to gain from the expertise of the sages—W. Edwards Deming, Peter Drucker, Napoleon Hill, Dale Carnegie, Tom Peters, Stephen Covey, Jim Collins, Jack Welch, Michael Gerber, David Maister, Dan Kennedy, Warren Bennis, and others. Thought leaders such as Daniel Goleman, Robert Kaplan and David Norton, John Kotter, Theodore Levitt, Michael Porter and others keep us on the leading edge of best business theories and practices. You must always be aware of and study their research, explore their ideas and test the application of their wisdom to your marketplace, even your life.

These thought leaders have a significant impact on the marketplace and it's a given that they still have much to teach us. I've certainly learned from them and continue to do so today. But, their books have already been written. Dan Kennedy—a significant influence on my thinking and performance—continues to publish and I appreciate his wisdom, perspective and encouragement.

I am also a sports enthusiast and I believe there are many transferable ideas from the playing field to the boardroom, so I add two names to this list—Bill Snyder and Robert Kraft. Snyder, legendary coach of Kansas State University, has to be the best football coach in the land. His book, *Leadership Lessons from Bill Snyder*, is packed with concepts that will help any business person, especially in turbulent times. Kraft, owner of the New England Patriots, has created an organization that is at the top of their game, respected for excellence by both friend and foe.

There are many good books describing the business acumen of Kraft, the Patriots' organization, and its highly successful coach, Bill Belichick. I recommend you observe and study the lessons that can be learned from Snyder and Kraft.

And since we're talking about the sages, there is a lesson in how W. Edwards Deming came to have a significant influence on my business thinking. On its face, Deming's work was primarily targeted at the manufacturing sector. His indictment of U.S. processes was severe. At the risk of oversimplifying, Deming's premise was that America's decline in international competitive advantage was due to a failure of management. Rather than focus on quarterly dividends and the stock price, companies, their employees and shareholders would be better off focusing on a constant improvement of the quality of product and service. Deming believed this change of focus would decrease costs, capture markets, provide jobs, and increase dividends. The work for which he is most known was centered on helping the auto industry in Japan in the 1950s and 1960s when those products were known for anything but quality.

Now the verdict is in. Toyota, despite recent challenges, dominates the industry and General Motors, a company that once had over a 50% market share, is a bankrupt partially state-owned enterprise that still owes U.S. taxpayers billions. A significant contribution to this development is because of higher than industry average costs. Another is low quality standards. The Japanese listened to, and more importantly, implemented many of Deming's ideas.

When I became a student of Deming's work light bulbs came on. As a former owner of community banks and the current owner of a professional services firm I could see how many of his ideas could be applied to my firm, to any business. The point of telling you this is that if you know Deming, Drucker and the others mentioned above, you will recognize their influence on my thinking and my belief system of how to achieve excellence in the business world.

This book is constructed to be all about how to conquer turbulence by creating a process-oriented business model and having the courage to take action. It is my hope you will gain new insights and be inspired to change behaviors. My objective is to show you how to convert these insights into practice, into new behaviors and better results for you and your business.

Bill Glazer, the former CEO and owner of Glazer-Kennedy Insider Circle, one of the largest information marketing businesses in the world and someone who has greatly influenced by thinking, says that one constant theme he hears is, "…but Bill, my business is different."

My response is the same as his—*nonsense*. Your specific deliverable might be different than mine, but the processes you use to create customers and satisfy them are remarkably similar.

As example, I've always viewed my law firm as a marketing company. We just happen to provide great legal services as the deliverable. Whether you are in a service, retail, manufacturing or distribution business, there are denominators common to all. Get your head trash out of the way and you'll learn much more from this book.

And finally, a couple of notes:

First, throughout the book I use "client" and "customer" interchangeably. I recommend you start thinking of those who purchase from you as clients. The term, itself, argues for a higher standard in the relationship.

The same goes for my use of the term "firm" or "company." Here, they are one and the same. Likewise for gender terminology. In today's world, the "she's" are just as fully engaged as business owners as the "he's" and in the end, turbulence doesn't discriminate... we're all in the same boat.

So, having given you the foundation, let's start to formulate our attack.

WHERE IT ALL
STARTED FOR ME...

My experience in the working world started at an early age. Albany, Missouri, was a small (population about 2,000—depending on how many travelers were passing through), agricultural county-seat town where everyone knew everyone. Those were the days of drug store fountain cherry cokes, jeans purchased three sizes too large, rolled up pant legs and stick-on patches when you tore a hole in the knee of your jeans. Until I started mowing yards, my Saturday morning entertainment was listening to the Lone Ranger and Dragnet on the radio. We didn't even have a television until around 1956.

But it was there that I learned that people and values matter... and it is a belief that I have carried with me ever since.

It was also here that I realized there was a "formula" for success. Watching my parents succeed year after year, despite meager economic beginnings, I realized that it was their burning desire to succeed that made that success possible. My parents did what many other families in my hometown did not: they expected to do better every year and had a vision for doing so. And with rare exception, they achieved their goals. I started to notice that the same could not be said of other families in Albany and that's when I began to study why some achieved more than others. That study continues today.

This book is a culmination of that study along with my own experiences along the way. I unofficially started my business career way back when, doing chores for an allowance, learning the value of earning my way, even if I didn't always enjoy the work itself. I went on to apply those ethics to the corporate world, working part-time for Columbia National Bank while attending the University of Missouri. There, I learned how to be an employee, to give more than I received and to work with others. In those early years I was lucky to work with and for great people.

It wasn't until 1982 that I took the plunge and opened my own business, followed in 1985 by the opening of my law firm while wrapping up other entrepreneurial ventures. The timing was poor. Penn Square Bank was shut down, the oil boom had gone bust and the agriculture business was suffering. Short term interest rates exceeded 20% and I did not escape the ripple effect. But it was a start... and it allowed the entrepreneurial spirit in me to grow.

In 1989, I read Michael Gerber's *The E-Myth* and realized what my entrepreneurial venture was missing. From that transformational moment, I ceased being the technician working in the business and instead, became the owner of the company working on the business. I came to understand that I didn't own a law firm — I owned a marketing company that happened to offer legal services as its product. I'm not in the business of making the thing; I'm in the business of marketing the thing.

This mindset has made an extraordinary contribution to my business success as have the experiences—some producing acceptable outcomes, others not—that I've had along the way. I've been a keen student of what we label as success and mistakes, my own and those of others, something I strongly recommend to anyone looking for insight.

By paying close attention to the world you live in, seeing the synapses connect, observing lessons in art, literature, sports and yes, even politics, you can gain tremendous perspective on what is required to be successful.

By the way, these are turbulent times. With the information age where "knowledge" is doubled every 18 months you should plan on turbulence being a permanent element of your business and life plan. In most industries it's all guerilla warfare out there. Whether you are a business owner, entrepreneur, professional or CEO of a large company, the days of hiding behind history, tradition, a unique product or bureaucratic structure are gone. Turbulence is here to stay . . . You are going to need to master these tools to be able to overcome it . . . to thrive . . . to achieve your dreams.

Enjoy the journey.

PART I
PHILOSOPHY
Finally... It Really
Is All About You

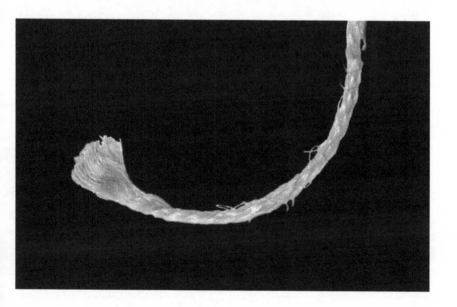

"The buck stops here."

— President Harry S. Truman

You Asked For It, Now Take It

You are about to embark on an exciting yet somewhat treacherous journey: you have decided to run your own business or are running one as its CEO. And just between us, getting to this point was the easy part.

Because when you accepted the task of becoming a CEO or starting or owning a business, you assumed an enormous responsibility—a responsibility that is yours and yours alone.

Finally—it truly is all about you!

Your dreams, your ideas… your concept of what success should look like. In fact, everything about this business will be a reflection of your vision… so if that vision isn't a clear one, or if your business is not turbulence-proof, it's your business that will suffer.

And therein lies the enormous responsibility we're talking about. After all, it's no longer just your personal success at stake, but the success of an entirely separate entity, as well. What's more, this entity isn't just a random storefront or a service or a product—instead, it's quite literally a part of you… a very significant part in fact, representing your vision of the "BIG PICTURE."

Add to this the fact that your core constituencies—clients, employees and vendors — will be relying on your vision to help fuel their own desires in one form or another. Now you can begin to grasp the significance of this undertaking. Your business will affect a large number of lives… and whether that effect is good or bad will be totally up to you.

It makes sense then, to give serious consideration to what it is you are trying to accomplish and more importantly, how you'll know when you've succeeded.

After all, no one else can define what success looks like for you, nor should they. This is your baby. Only you can say if it's working or not — and if it isn't, it's up to you to decide how to move forward.

And that's not always an easy thing to do. Having a business idea is one thing but when you bring that idea to life, it often takes off and evolves on its own. Sometimes the evolution is exactly what you had in mind and sometimes, it's not, but you'll be held accountable regardless because… well… you're in charge.

See? It really is all about you.

So, given that your backside is clearly on the line, you'll probably want to do everything you can to ensure your business thrives. But since it's also a given that you'll be building your company during turbulent times, you can bet that achieving that success will require more than just good intentions.

Whether it's our struggling economy or the ever-changing landscape of the digital age, the marketplace simply isn't what it used to be and being in charge requires much more than just hanging your shingle out for the world to see.

In short, the days of just showing up are over.

In fact, it is during turbulent times that the performance grade cards are handed out. After all, it's easy to be successful when times are good. It was easy for financial advisors to hold themselves out as experts during the bull market run from 2001 to 2008… but we didn't truly know if they were worth their fees until they met the bear. That could be said of any of us. We are never as good as we think and it's overcoming the challenges that allow us to sow the seeds of long-term success.

So, rather than retreat or bury our heads in the sand during turbulent times as many business owners often and mistakenly do, we should ascend to the castle and arm ourselves with the attitudes, processes and resources that enable us to not just survive the tumult around us, but to thrive and prosper regardless which way the tide turns.

And it's these attitudes, processes and resources we'll talk about here.

No matter how different you think your business might be, at the heart of every CEO and business owner is a common denominator: they share the rare alchemy of the entrepreneur. In today's world, adaptation is key; it doesn't matter if you're the CEO of General Electric, a company that migrated from light bulbs to turbine engines to finance to green energy; or the owner of a growing small business in Northwest Missouri — the challenge is the same: we must keep our business proposition relevant in the marketplace. And that requires, now more than ever, the heart of an entrepreneur.

In his book, *The Theory of Economic Development*, author Joseph Schumpeter talks about this spirit. He says, "First of all, there is the dream and the will to found a private kingdom, usually, though not necessarily, also a dynasty... Then there is the will to conquer: the impulse to fight, to prove oneself superior to others, to succeed for the sake, not of the fruits of success, but of success itself... Finally, there is the joy of creating, of getting things done, or simply of exercising one's energy and ingenuity."

That sentence was recently reprinted in a Wall Street Journal editorial (Wall Street Journal, August 26, 2011) in response to Steve Jobs' announcement that he was stepping down as Apple's CEO. I'm sure you'll agree that it adequately describes the intensity Jobs brought to executing his vision of Apple. So then, the question is, can you bring an equal intensity to your business to achieve your desired outcomes? Will you? As Deming would ask, "By what method?"

So, since this is truly all about you—and today it takes you at your best, every day—I think it's only fitting that we start with a few key attitudes of leaders and achievers who have thrived in both good times and bad, turbulence notwithstanding.

12 Tenets of Successful Business Owners

It would be easier if I referred to what business owners and CEOs exhibit in carrying out their business and personal missions as attributes. Instead, I prefer to refer to them as attitudes or "tenets," because when you get right down to it, these qualities are in fact, the foundation of their belief systems. And let's be honest — we're all aware of the direct and irrefutable link of attitude, belief and outcome.

Tony Robbins has an interesting model that makes this point. Rather than classifying himself as a motivational speaker, Tony sees himself as someone who helps others get to and operate from what he refers to as "peak state"…making him their peak performance coach. His goal is to find out what people do when they are operating at their peak and then show them how to access that same peak state, on demand.

Of course, if you asked ten leaders to name their top five tenets, you might get 50 different answers. However, as I've worked with these leaders in coaching programs and consulting engagements, I've notice that there are a few key attitudes that reveal themselves with great frequency and intensity in high achievers. It is these twelve I want to share with you now:

COURAGE

Perhaps the most valuable attitude on this list, courage is abundant among the movers and shakers. This is not reckless, mind you; it's just focused action taken in the face of doubt or overwhelming odds. It should not be confusing then, why courage tops this list — courage causes one to act when most would not.

Business leaders spend a considerable amount of their time dealing with issues that are not black and white, and few of those decisions are easy. It takes tremendous courage for a business owner to pursue a strategy that requires him to guarantee a $200 thousand or $200 million loan at the bank. It takes an equal amount of courage to fire a long-time employee who has performed with excellence in the past, but now fails to meet your standards. More critically, courage is often most difficult to demonstrate during the times of our greatest crisis, during turbulent times when outcomes are at the apogee of uncertainty.

Case in point: during the late 1990's, I was serving on the advisory board of a privately owned public affairs/public relations firm in Washington, D.C. In 2001, the market was hot and larger firms in the industry were in a consolidation mode, often paying owners of boutique firms large multiples of income to buy their business. Seeing an opportunity, the company's owner informed the board he would like to sell the company and the board responded that there were substantial steps required before the company could be presented to a buyer in the most favorable light.

A few weeks later the owner, who I had known for over 25 years, approached me and asked if I would consider making a move to D.C., assume responsibility as president of the firm and help him get it ready for sale. I hesitated for a few weeks, uncertain of whether it would be a good fit, for him and for me. Our previous working relationship in a political campaign years before had proved challenging. Both of us are strong-willed, not easily swayed and very determined. Those skirmishes had been pretty intense and we both knew the risks. In the final analysis, I came home one night, looked at my wife and said, "The kids are gone and the dog's dead. Let's go do this. We'll be home in three years."

So, I took a three-year sabbatical from my law firm, moved to D.C. and became president of the firm. A few months later, 9/11 ripped at the soul of our country and at the economic core of many companies. Our firm was not immune and within 60 days, we lost 25% of our revenue. But I had two things on my side: I had a great CFO, excellent at accurate historic and prognostic number-crunching, and I knew how important it was to take swift action in the face of adversity.

I knew the kind of courage required to do what has to be done when the firm's survival is at stake, no matter how painful it might be. Most business owners, CEOs and entrepreneurs develop emotional ties to their position, their people and their strategies. Breaking those ties can be the most difficult challenge confronting a business leader, especially during adversity.

This firm and its owner was no exception. Shortly after the 9/11 attack, a number of us were standing on the roof of our office building in Alexandria, Virginia watching smoke billowing from the Pentagon strike. It was clear to me my mission was going to change. I was brought there to help sell the firm. Now I was going to be tasked with helping save it.

I had faced economic trauma in the mid-1980s. Those were lessons I would never forget. Now I was responsible for managing financial trauma for someone else suffering through it. Because our businesses tend to become a significant element of our self-worth, it is nearly impossible to separate the business crisis and your personal life. I know the symptoms of a crisis in the making. I can sense the overwhelming power of fear and see how it dominates one's thinking process a mile away. No one is immune. Harvard graduate degrees do not include an inoculation against a loss of courage in the face of adversity.

Addressing the issue of courage with the owner became almost as big a challenge as the economic challenge faced by the firm. Denial reigned, but thank goodness it did not persist. In the end, most of the changes that were needed were made, owner resistance notwithstanding. He knew that failure to act with courage to deal with survival issues would be as deadly as an encounter with a tsunami. In a crisis, the action you have to take will always exceed what you plan or want to take. This is a lesson on courage worth remembering.

ADVENTUROUS

A first cousin of Courage is the willingness to go where others fear to tread. In our free enterprise system, our future belongs to thoughtful risk takers — we just need government to remove the shackles. Successful business owners and CEOs not only see opportunity, they sense it. Their 360 degree opportunity tentacles are so alert in fact, that when they sense an idea is aligning with their vision, they rapidly move to learn more and then with little evidence, they often begin to act and implement.

Many take risk after risk, often to the point of depleting capital and human resources, in pursuit of their dream. They achieve great rewards and they also experience colossal setbacks, often accompanied by embarrassment, even ridicule. This can make it difficult to get others to follow you and help you get to where you know you need to go, but the true leader understands the importance of inspiring change in the face of risk. In a risk-based environment, acting in an adventurous manner can be challenging. It often triggers the "what in the world is he doing now" syndrome.

CarterEnergy Corporation's CEO, Bryan Beaver, compares this to being the lead dog on the sled. "When you're the lead dog," he says, "you're vulnerable and at risk because you're leading the whole pack—all running hard and fast—down a different path. If you want to drive change—if you want to lead them down that new path — you have to inspire the team to go with you."

If you are adventurous you have to be better at managing change and the people experiencing it with you. You can't simply implement the changes with force—especially in turbulent times—because you'll lose your team in the process. Instead, you have to make your team *want to follow you*, so that everyone travels smoothly into that new direction.

And as Bryan points out, that kind of leadership is an art form all its own.

VISION

We're going to talk quite a bit about vision a little later but for now, just know that it's a must if you want to succeed as an entrepreneur. Having vision means you know where you're going… not just today, tomorrow or even next month, but years down the line. Hockey great Wayne Gretsky attributed his success to his ability to skate where the puck was going to be… not where it was currently located. Vision is your version of the big picture opportunities—both those that exist today and in the future. And people who have this attribute seem to build all the other areas of their lives around it to support it.

That's because your vision represents not just the money you want to make or the fame you want to attain, but also your core beliefs about life, success and purpose. In fact, your vision IS your purpose—it's what drives you to get out of bed and it's what you dream about when you let your imagination have some fun.

In Peter Drucker's version of the classic stonecutter story, a traveler happens upon three men cutting stone. The traveler asks them what they're doing and the first man replies, "I am making a living." The second man replies, "I am cutting stone better than anyone else in the whole country." And the third man replies, "I am building a cathedral."

In the first man's vision, he saw his work as a means to an end... that is, he wanted fair pay for fair labor. The second man's vision was focused only on his own growth and improvement, something that Drucker considered to be the most problematic of the three. And, then the third man saw far beyond the first two and envisioned the cathedral that would be built with the stones he cut.

So, you have to ask yourself... Where is your focus? What does your vision include? And are you making a living or building cathedrals?

In the business world, that vision is what will give your company direction and meaning. Your employees will look to you for guidance on which way to move... it's your vision that provides those answers.

KNOWLEDGEABLE

It's said that at the beginning of every Green Bay Packers' summer camp, even the ones following a NFL championship season or Super Bowl victory, the legendary coach, Vince Lombardi, would sit the players in a semi-circle, hold up a football and say, "Gentlemen, this is a football." The moral of that story is that success in any competitive environment usually goes to the team that has most completely mastered the fundamentals.

In business, those fundamentals are equally important. Mastery of the knowledge of the fundamentals can help your team stay focused on true worth in the midst of chaos and turbulence. Like the players need to recognize the football, a business owner needs to master every aspect of their company or firm. You must know the processes and systems within the organization like the back of your hand. You must have a clear understanding of cost, pricing, marketing, sales drivers, staffing capabilities and needs, as well as the financial requirements to achieve desired results. You must know the strengths of your organization and the advantages your company has over its competitors.

In short, you need know which actions influence or lead to bottom line results. That requires knowing every aspect of your business... every nook and cranny, if you want to withstand today's marketplace turmoil. You must be knowledgeable beyond the unknown degree and here's a quick exercise to demonstrate where that kind of knowledge can take you:

Imagine taking your profit and loss statement, starting at the bottom then working your way up through every single line item, considering the complex webs of how each one influences the other, finally reaching the top line revenue — and then turning your analysis into actions that created that top line number and the behaviors required to take those actions. Now you're being creative and becoming knowledgeable!

By the way, this is how I build next year's budget—from the bottom up, not from the top down. You start with profit targets and then work your way upward until you have to calculate the action required to generate the revenue that supports the organization you just erected.

The reason is this: knowing your business gives you a clear understanding of how it interacts with the surrounding environment. This allows you to adapt to the ever-changing landscape of the business world, making adjustments where necessary to ensure your company or firm continues to meet the needs of your target market.

Now, there are several ways to get a handle on the environmental fundamentals and we'll take a look at how best to do this analysis later in the book. But for now, just start thinking about the different positions and processes in your company—do you have mastery-type knowledge of each and every one?

PRESENT FOCUSED, FUTURE DIRECTED

Last spring, I attended a first round NBA playoff game between the Los Angeles Lakers and Oklahoma City Thunder. It was the first play-off appearance for the young Thunder team. During a TV time-out, there was a commercial sponsored by the league. A few NBA stars were interviewed about the playoff atmosphere. Over and over they kept saying one word: *focus. We just have to focus, remember why we're here.*

And you're mantra should be the same. A good leader in any field understands the importance of focus. But what do you focus on? The tasks at hand or your visions of that golden future?

The truth is, there will always be a natural tension between being focused on the present and looking forward to the future. Balancing these two timelines is crucial to your success. In 1980, Roberto Goizueta became CEO of Coca-Cola, proclaiming there would be no sacred cows, including how the company formulated its drinks. At the time, the company was losing market share and it was decided that they needed a sweeter tasting drink to stall Pepsi's growth. A few years later, Goizueta led a drive to change the formula and taste of the company's flagship cola. Despite prior taste tests indicating a preference for New Coke, it was a marketing fiasco. In 1992, the company corrected their strategy by introducing Coke Classic, the original formula that had carried them for so many years.

Goizueta and his team were indeed willing to take risks but they placed too much focus on where they were going and lost sight of what they had going for them right now. And while both present focus and future direction are critical, this example demonstrates the risk of over-emphasizing one to the exclusion of the other.

ADAPTABILITY

Some people prefer a life of black and white. In the business world, that rarely exists and when it does, astute leaders exhibit a healthy skepticism, wondering what they're missing.

That's because they know that ambiguity and complexity have become the norm in today's business world. They've learned to expect the unexpected.

The Information Age changed everything. It creates a never-ending tsunami-like shift in consumer buying patterns and preferences. It changes the way we market our products and it redefines the way we connect with our market. It sets off a new wave of processes and strategies for every element of business — manufacturing, operations, IT, marketing, sales and service all included — in virtually every industry in the world.

Yet ironically, in the face of all this complexity, it's simplicity that most of my business clients are looking for. They want us to show them how to manage all this complexity in a simple and straightforward way. And that's true whether we're dealing with law firm clients or clients in our executive development and coaching firm.

Unfortunately, this is easier said than done. To use another sports metaphor, football was once dominated by a "three yards and a cloud of dust" approach. Darrell Royal, the former coach at the University of Texas, liked to keep things simple. His teams were extraordinarily successful at executing the wishbone offense—they ran the ball . . . and ran it some more. Likewise for Barry Switzer at Oklahoma. Coach Royal used to say that when you pass, only three things can happen and two of them are bad. My, how that game has changed. In today's game, they sling the ball all over the field, utilizing the entire field to create mismatches and competitive advantage. Complexity reigns.

And, how about the game of baseball? There used to be a starting pitcher and a reliever. Now we have a starter good for six-seven innings, a mid-inning reliever, a late inning reliever and a closer, the guy who specializes in "saves." To measure productivity we kept track of a hitter's batting average, RBIs, home runs, on base percentages and slugging percentages. Now you need a computer and software program to calculate the stats kept by teams and the fantasy leagues.

Our business lives are no different. I refer to this as the paradox of competing priorities. Nothing is as easy or simple as we would like and nearly every decision is a complex matter. Recently I was informed that one of our clients had passed away. He'd been with us for over 20 years; I knew him well and wanted to attend his funeral. But I also had calls scheduled with four of our Peak Performer coaching participants for that same morning, leaving me in a bit of a bind. Does one take precedence over the other? How do I decide? This is just one example of the millions of conflicts that occur every day for business owners and CEOs.

To successfully lead and grow a business you must deal with and effectively govern ambiguity and complexity or, as Bryan Beaver says, "You have to learn to get comfortable with being uncomfortable." When I work with clients to help them with their business issues, one of the first things I do is determine their ceiling of complexity. Their comfort with strategic complexities influences my recommendations. And incidentally, I've found that if we never lose touch with the fundamentals, the ambiguities and complexities have less of a chance to obscure the mission.

So, exactly how does one learn to deal with constant ambiguity and complexity? According to Alterra Bank Chairman, Mick Aslin, that's where confidence comes in. He adds that when there's no more black and white and you're not sure which way is up, you have to fall back on what you know, what you believe. And if you've mastered your fundamentals, you'll have the confidence to move forward, even when the playing field is unfamiliar.

One final thought about the paradox of complexity and simplicity: you need simplicity so team members can readily understand and quickly apply practices required to succeed. But, the only way you can achieve that simplicity is by going through the rigors of complex analysis. It requires a careful, detailed analysis of each contributing element of the task at hand. In effect, you need a mini-plan for each step in order to arrive at the destination of simplicity.

COMMITTED TO CONTINUOUS IMPROVEMENT

Early in my career, I had the opportunity to work in the Investment Division of United Missouri Bank in Kansas City. The Investment Division was headed by Byron Thompson. Byron was, and remains to this day, a legend in the banking and investment community. Over the years, I'm sure he has been pleased with many of his accomplishments as there have been a number of them, both professionally and personally and within his family.

Yet one of Byron's greatest attitudes is that he is never quite satisfied. When things weren't going well, he was supportive and encouraging. And when things running smoothly, he constantly reminded us that we weren't nearly as good as we thought...that there was so much more we could be doing. "Look closer," he said, "and find a way to do better." Byron was reminding us that there was always room to improve and for achievers, this is the language of inspiration and motivation.

A YES, NOW ATTITUDE

While it's true that the most effective business leaders say yes a lot, a more accurate statement is that they say, "Yes, but do your homework."

That's because once they say yes, they want it done quickly... as in yesterday, meaning that you need to have a plan and be ready to take action once the green light has been given. As a trader of fixed income securities at United Missouri Bank, I knew that if I wanted to take positions so we could buy and sell in the same market, I had to move quickly. Otherwise, you're speculating. Markets move fast and the logical decision could become obsolete in mere moments.

The same is true in today's business world. Decisions made today have often been researched for months. They have the benefit of input from a number of people inside and outside of the organization. They are budgeted to fit those assumptions. Yet, assumption can change within a matter of minutes and the entire basis of the decision becomes invalid. If that decision triggered a strategy in the marketplace that included a commitment of serious financial resources, then the entire campaign is at risk and at the very least, subject to falling short of projections. At worst, it could fail completely and put your company's future at risk.

Like a successful trader who must buy and sell in the same market, a successful CEO has to implement fast to be sure her assumptions have the longest possible shelf life in the marketplace.

Of the many excellent qualities of martial arts master and real estate mogul, Lloyd Irvin, his most impressive is that he gets things done…fast. He accomplishes this by creating an internal sense of urgency for task completion. Irvin imagines his family held captive, destined to die if he does not complete the task by the self-imposed deadline. You may think that's a bit extreme, but it works for him and I can assure you Lloyd Irvin gets things done. He is a person seriously committed to fast implementation with excellence.

PROMISE KEEPERS

This might seem like an obvious attribute to include, but it is critically important. This tenet goes to the heart of dependability and trust, two characteristics that help form the foundation of success in the midst of turbulence and chaos.

And I have a personal example to prove my point. I recently walked by the work area of one of our key team members. She normally has a wonderful attitude and disposition, so you can understand my surprise when she seemed a little out of sorts. Clearly, she was disappointed about something.

As it turned out, two weeks earlier she had scheduled a meeting with one of our attorneys to review nearly two pages of pending client matters. He had been reminded that morning yet showed up 30 minutes late anyway and by that time, both had to get ready for the next appointment, so very little got accomplished. As a result, a key employee felt unimportant and completely discounted because the attorney hadn't treated their meeting with the respect it deserved. At that point, he failed as a Promise Keeper.

Unfortunately, this happens frequently in the business world. Yes, schedules have to be adjusted and sometimes delays simply can't be avoided, but there's a way to handle those adjustments without diminishing the needs of those working with you and around you. What should have been a productive and results-driven meeting instead turned out to be a de-motivator for a key employee and another delay in resolving important client matters. As Robert Armstrong, one of my coaching colleagues says, how someone does one thing is how they do everything. If someone acting in the capacity of a leader repeats this behavior too often, respect and trust will be lost. Any remaining leadership will be exercised entirely on authority, not influence. Even worse, you begin the process of destroying the soul of a committed team member.

Keeping promises applies to those made to fellow team members, clients, family members or other professionals. In our coaching groups, there are often actions identified which need to be taken in order to move a participant toward a stated goal. Once we identify the next action I usually ask, "When will you report this as accomplished?" The participants set the date. Sometimes they miss it but if it happens more than once, I know we need to have a different conversation.

Being a Promise Keeper means making good on your commitments, even if those commitments have been dimmed by time or perceived importance. George Zalucki once said, "Commitment is doing the thing you said you would do long after the mood you said it in has passed." That's also a good definition of a Promise Keeper.

In my experience, keeping your promises is right up there with courage on the list of must-have attributes for success. Keeping to your word instills confidence—people know they can depend on you and trust you to do what you say you're going to do. It's a quality that speaks to the very core of who you are as a human being. You can never become a leader of an organization or a key member of an organization's team if your word is a bottomless bucket.

DECISIVE

As the boss, you'll be expected to make decisions. Yet, there's more to being decisive than just saying yes or no.

Being an effective leader means that you'll make decisions regardless of the circumstances. It means that you'll use all the tools and resources you have at your disposal to find the right answer and when that doesn't work, you'll go with your gut and make a decision. It means that you'll make the hard decisions as well as the easy ones . . . that you'll take responsibility for those decisions and that you'll stand behind the people that carry them out on your behalf.

Being decisive does not mean you're impetuous. It means that you temper your desire to get ahead and grow your bottom line with everything that's good and right...honorable...that your decisions are made with compassion and respect... never from ego and emotion. It means that you prepare and when it's time to act, you embrace the opportunity.

Top athletes want the ball in their hands at decision time. Michael Jordon almost always insisted on taking the last shot to win a game. The higher the stakes, the more he insisted. And, remember the play-off game when he forfeited the last shot, passed the ball out to a wide open Steve Kerr who hit the winning shot? That's about taking responsibility and being decisive.

No, you won't hit every game winning shot. Neither did Michael Jordon. But like him, you'll learn from your mistakes. Never let regret, confusion or uncertainty cloud your ability to be decisive in the future.

CREATIVE

In a 2010 study by IBM, creativity was pegged as the most important leadership quality to achieve success in the coming years. Not integrity, not discipline or strategic thinking... creativity.

Want to know why?

Because in a world where competition is fierce and markets are turbulent, leaders must be willing to break the boundaries of the "norm" and move outside the status quo. And that means you need some creativity in your CEO arsenal. Being creative allows you to see the bigger picture. It allows you to find new ways of succeeding, and it gives you the option of creating something new instead of just overcoming obstacles to meet existing demands.

If you closely examine examples where huge wealth has been created over the past few years, you'll notice they were often created from nothing. I mean nothing more than an idea. The creator didn't try for incremental improvement. They created entirely new categories. They thought far beyond to the realm of creating something previously unavailable or non-existent. Think Microsoft, Apple, fracking and horizontal drilling in the oil and gas business, Facebook and other businesses. All of them, without exception, did something new. Ask this question—who made the rule that says you have to . . . ?

A simple example: In our law firm we offer estate planning, business succession planning and elder law solutions. Pretty traditional, right? To those capabilities, we added comprehensive financial services and business consulting and coaching. And, we use an employee in India and numerous other outsourced vendors from all over the world to help us accomplish our mission. That's very unusual, if not unique, in the world of boutique law firms.

In a nutshell, being creative—in origination or application—will set you apart from competitors and reveal a path to success that others might not be able to see; or be unwilling to adopt.

AUTHENTIC

I'm going to fudge just a little with this last one. Being authentic actually encompasses a few different characteristics. On their own, each of these traits would certainly be an admirable quality. But it's when you bundle them together — as I'm about to do here — that you begin to see their real power.

Being authentic first means you have integrity, as in you're an honest, honorable, stand-up kind of person . . . someone who people can trust to do the right thing and make the right choices, even and especially when doing so is not popular or easy.

Authentic leaders are also driven. They have no choice but to go forward. It's embedded into their DNA. They embrace the uncertainty, the stress and the risk because they love the journey itself and they can't imagine sitting still. In fact, it's when things become stagnant that they become uncomfortable and true to form, they'll shake things up just to start moving again.

Finally, an authentic leader becomes a natural leader, meaning that others actually *choose* to follow them — not because they were told to and not because they fear what will happen if they don't. No, they follow you because you inspire them . . . and they believe in your ability to lead and more importantly, to achieve results.

Again, these aren't the only qualities that make a good leader. You could easily add credibility, self-sufficiency, empathetic, competitive and results-oriented for example, and still have room to add more.

But that's the thing about being a successful CEO, business owner or entrepreneur... it's not just one quality that distinguishes this unique personality from the rest of the pack. They possess all these traits and more.

And it's this combination that makes them so exciting to be around. Because an entrepreneur isn't just someone who knows how to take advantage of an opportunity... an entrepreneur is someone who can create those opportunities where none existed before.

CAUTION:
OBSTACLES AHEAD!

Having read my definition of what it takes to be a successful entrepreneur, I'm going to take the fact that you're still here as an indication that you believe you've got what it takes.

But while qualities like courage and confidence can certainly give you a running start, those same qualities will also ensure that you hit a few snags along the way. After all, it's in your nature to be optimistic and see the possibilities in every situation. Yes, you may be good at seeing the downside as well but at your core, you believe you can make something work and in most cases, you can do it in record time and with stellar results.

If you didn't, you wouldn't be here.

But this belief can also be your undoing. For example, confidence can gradually become arrogance. Many have never drawn the line that separates hubris and confidence. Your willingness to take risks can turn into recklessness if you don't keep it in check. And then suddenly, the strengths that brought you to where you are now become the trigger that causes your downfall.

Fortunately, just as there are certain traits that you'll need to be successful, there are also certain behaviors you'll want to avoid.

THE NEED TO BE RIGHT

Let's face it: you didn't get to where you are now by missing the mark, so it stands to reason that you've enjoyed being right more than just a few times. But this ability isn't infallible and you're not the only one on your team with ideas.

Unfortunately for many CEOs, that couldn't be further from the truth. They've grown so accustomed to being the one with the ideas and solutions that they come to rely on it... even insist upon it, and it's not long before their staff figures out how to tell them exactly what they want to hear. If everyone around you is chirping, ". . . that sounds great," at your every utterance, you are in trouble and don't even know it.

And when this happens, you're no longer leading effectively. In fact, you're no longer leading at all. Just to set the record straight, as a business owner or CEO, your job is to see that the business strategy is executed. It's not your job to come up with a new, great idea every day and it's certainly not your job to "do" each and every task required of effective execution.

UNDERESTIMATING THE DIFFICULTY OF THE TASK

The same ego that insists on being right all the time can also convince you that you can do things better or faster than they can really be done. This is called underestimating the difficulty of your task and it's a phenomenon so common that it's a regular topic in marketing guru Dan Kennedy's coaching sessions.

The problem is our ego—coupled with the excitement of starting something new — makes it difficult to look past the potential and evaluate a project or task realistically. Ego says not only can it be done, but we're exactly the right person for the job: And because listening to this inner voice has proved to be fruitful in the past, it's hard to discount its optimism now.

As a result, we'll predict a better than average outcome because we've learned to rely heavily on our "Can Do!" mentality. But when we're unable to meet those expectations, the consequences can wreak all kinds of havoc in our otherwise productive world.

Underestimating fosters procrastination for example, encouraging us to put off the big projects in the belief that there's plenty of time to complete it later. It also causes us to fall short of our customers' expectations and when this happens consistently, our company's reputation suffers as a result.

Underestimating task difficulty is compounded by failing to prioritize. In one of our recent weekly marketing meetings, we found ourselves having déjà vu conversations while reviewing our priorities, project updates and future plans. These conversations we realized, sounded much like the ones we had the week before, two weeks before and even a month before.

Important projects—many of our top priorities—had gone stale. They were stagnated… dead in the water, and all because we had failed to prioritize. And we had failed to prioritize because we had underestimated the difficulty of the projects we had taken on.

Now, "difficulty" doesn't just refer to the complexity of the task in question. It can also manifest as a lack of time, inappropriate allocation of resources or money to a project. It knows no boundaries, is indiscriminate in its targets and attacks from angles previously unseen.

There is a story that illustrates how setting priorities can slow down a project. It was demonstrated to me when in training to instruct the Dale Carnegie Leadership/Management program. The instructor-trainer took out a glass container, set it on the table along with four large rocks, a handful of smaller rocks, separate piles of gravel and sand, and a pitcher of water. He asked one of the participants to come to the front of the room and put all of these items into the glass container. Failure. I'm thinking he wouldn't be conducting this exercise unless it could be done, right? How will this material go into the container? No way…too much to fit in. A few others tried but with no success. Then he showed us the way.

He put the largest rocks in first. The smaller ones followed. Gravel came next, followed by sand. Finally, he poured every last ounce of that pitcher into the container. Perfect fit. And he did it quickly.

Of course, his point was that in order to reach your objective you have to focus on the big rocks first…know what's most important and move those to the top of your list. Tackle first those that make the greatest contribution, have the greatest impact on moving you toward your goals or completion of your project, and then start working down from there.

But be careful. Even with the Big Rock Practice firmly in place, it's easy to get side-tracked. Remembering *Seven Habits of Highly Successful People*, we learned that working in the Urgent but Not Important quadrant is destructive. Others refer to it as "the tyranny of the urgent."

This is one important reason we don't get our projects completed on time or within budget. We get side-tracked by bright-shiny objects that appear more urgent and more important. We become reactive, not proactive. And our productivity suffers as a result.

Yesterday, I sat in a meeting with a young man who was presenting his services to us. Our telephone interview with him had been encouraging. We were optimistic he was our solution to a project that had been derailed far too long. But during the meeting, he insisted on checking his phone every time it vibrated in his pocket. This of course, interrupted our conversation as well as the productive energy of the meeting. Sale over, time wasted. And all because he couldn't give us the focus that we needed.

The point of these examples is that all priorities, projects and actions take longer and prove more challenging than we originally estimate. Don't undermine your efforts by making behavior mistakes like the young phone addict. This is one reason people participate in our mastermind and coaching programs. They are committed to results and are willing to accept encouragement and accountability from others that they either cannot or will not provide for themselves. Find your own ways to stay focused on implementing the big rocks and becoming the exception to this powerful, destructive rule.

Of course, we don't want to believe that we've underestimated the project, so instead we'll place blame somewhere else—on the employees that didn't perform for example, or the vendors that didn't deliver. But in the end, it doesn't matter who's at fault because the result is still the same: your company's reputation is tarnished and your employees no longer see you in the same light.

And a company like that won't last long.

DOING IT THE WAY YOU'VE ALWAYS DONE IT

This challenge is endemic in all businesses with any history, but there may be no better example than the legal profession. As an attorney, I can safely tell you that my profession was slow to fully embrace the benefits of the digital revolution, and even slower to recognize the reality of intense marketplace competition. We've never had to worry about those things before, so why start now? And because of this mentality, the legal profession continues to insulate itself from competition even today. It's a completely closed system, still using hourly billing as its business model, passing on inefficiency and ineffectiveness to the client. Until recently, there was little incentive for the profession to change. Why get things done fast when we can move slowly and charge more? We even resisted emails and websites as long as we possibly could, hoping against hope that all this online marketing stuff would just somehow go away. And even now, when it's clear that the virtual world isn't going anywhere, there are still plenty of lawyers out there ignoring the evidence that tells them to take their business online.

And that's a behavior you'll want to avoid.

What worked yesterday may not work today and what works tomorrow may be something else altogether. To be an effective leader, you have to pay serious attention to the changing dynamics of the marketplace and then be willing to grow with your market by adapting your services and products to the changing needs of your customers. Sticking to your core principles and holding fast to your mission is one thing — but when you sacrifice growth and profitability because it requires change, you're not leading. You are hiding behind the curtain of caution and you are killing your company.

FAILING TO DELEGATE

Just because you're in charge now doesn't mean that this was always the case. In fact, if you're like most CEOs, you probably have a list of jobs and life experiences a mile long. Because of that, you've acquired a nice collection of excellent skills . . . skills that enable you to perform a variety of tasks, even those you no longer need to do.

But for some business owners, it's hard to let go. After all you can do it faster and better, right?

It's not just that you know how to do a certain task, it's that you know how to do it very well and in the time it would take you to train someone to do it with equal satisfaction, you could've done it yourself....twice.

But holding onto all the responsibility makes it hard for you to lead. After all, if you're busy drafting the contracts, making sales calls, working "on the line" and filling the orders, when will you have time to analyze your competitive advantage, consider new products and strategize a new marketing campaign, all while seeing that effective execution is taking place throughout the organization?

Failing to delegate also makes it hard for your employees to grow. If you're never allowing them new challenges and new responsibilities, it won't be long before they become bored and stagnant. They will resent the fact you don't let them do their job. And, when that happens morale will suffer and you can bet your company will head off in the wrong direction.

DELEGATING THE WRONG THING

Just as you can not delegate enough, you can also delegate too much and/or give away the wrong things. This is the other extreme of delegation and it can become dangerous territory especially, according to Dan Kennedy, when you take yourself entirely out of the task.

According to Dan, there are two things that should *never be delegated*:

One is the checkbook. Anybody that isn't at least looking at and signing all their own checks is doing the equivalent of putting a great big roll of hundred dollar bills visibly in their pocket, wearing a Rolex on their arm and strolling around in the dark alleys of the worst section in town. You may get away with that once or twice, but if you're going to do that every night for a handful of years, you're most certainly going to get mugged.

The second thing that you should never totally delegate is the top tasks that actually produce and keep the customers and bring in the profits. Very often, business owners come to be owners because they were first technicians in the field. The lawyer worked for somebody else before he had his own practice just as the auto repair guy fixed cars as a mechanic before he owned his own garage.

"We call this the 'be-your-own-boss' ground," says Dan. "He really still wants to be a mechanic. He just doesn't want a boss telling him when to go to lunch or take vacation. That's his vision when he goes into business."

Of course, as we've already established, owning a business isn't always what you think it's going to be and often, business owners begin delegating tasks they don't want to do. But "the truth is, they have to become the chief marketing officer, whether they like it or not… and until they make that shift, their income is going to be very limited and erratic."

MICROMANAGING YOUR TEAM

This is the twin sister of failing to delegate. Now, that we've established the importance of delegating, let's talk about the importance of letting go.

After team members have been trained and feedback systems are in place, giving new responsibilities to your staff works best if you also give them the freedom to do the job you've hired them to do. Unfortunately, many CEOs and certainly many mid-level managers, feel the need to keep their hand in everything, micromanaging every project and every task to ensure that things get done right. That's because they failed to adequately train and test competency before turning a team member loose. "Here, go do it," is not a training program. Rest assured Coach Snyder doesn't practice a play once and say, "Okay, we've got it." So, why would you?

Once trained, stepping back and giving your staff room to grow gives you the opportunity to evaluate just how far they've come. It gives you the chance to see how they cope in new situations, a concept that we'll discuss more a little later on. Yes, they will falter from time to time and you should build that assumption into their development. Pick them up, discuss lessons learned, review benchmarks again and move on. No one ever learned to ride a bicycle without falling down. Get them back on the bike. Keep getting better. What is it about this we don't get?

It also allows your employees to learn from their mistakes—just as you learned from yours. And that's a lesson that is crucial to the growth of your company.

CHARTING YOUR COURSE

With a sound philosophy in place, you might think you're ready to charge forward and lead your company to great things… but not just yet.

Remember, you're in charge of this sailing ship so the crew will look to you to chart a course… and that course needs to be one that embraces everything you've imagined your company or firm should be. That means you need a clear idea of where it is you want to go. It means that you need some detailed milestones that will take you to the destination of your choice. And it means that you need some potential options for Plan B if Plan A turns out to be a bust.

In short, it means you need a plan.

In the next section, we're going to show you how to create such a plan. Before we do, I want to cover one more essential element for your success: influence.

It doesn't matter how creative you are, how powerful you are, how persuasive or charming or smart you are… without influence, you can't lead and if you can't lead, you'll never reach your goal. Because your company can't go any farther than you can take it.

In his book, *The 21 Irrefutable Laws of Leadership*, author and international speaker John Maxwell calls this the Law of Influence — measuring your ability to lead and your ability to effect change. This is a good place to pause, take out a notebook and make that assessment.

What kind of change can you affect simply by influencing people to follow you? If you don't like the answer to this question, then now is the time to start changing it. Influence is gained not just by your knowledge or experience or ability, but by these things and more. Influence is based on trust—that is, others must trust you before they'll agree to follow. Once trust is established, they must also believe in the course you've charted.

And it's up to you to establish that trust and affirm those beliefs.

Circle back to the idea of being a Promise Keeper. To do this, you'll have to lead by example, enticing others to join you by showing them the passion and commitment you have to the company and its goals. They need to see your sacrifice before they'll be willing to make one of their own. They need to witness your dedication before they'll give you their loyalty. And they need to believe in your purpose before they'll follow your path.

And this is something that only you can do. As you analyze your situation within your company ask yourself: How do I measure up? How would others say I measure up? What specific steps can I take to strengthen my position on the influence issue?

Answer those questions and then take actions that will improve those answers. Because in the end, if you can't influence those you're leading, then you're not really leading at all.

Some Final Thoughts on the Philosophy

There is a significant body of work suggesting we should operate from our strengths. If you are not utilizing your strengths in your current situation it will be difficult to maintain the excitement and enthusiasm required for significant achievement. It will be a challenge to wake up in the morning and get busy on the task at hand. Soon, your professional life, then your personal life, will become a dreary place. For me, the commitment to build a business that utilizes my strengths and does not consume me with working on things that are not my strengths, is one of the first pieces of advice that I would offer to anyone. Find out what you're good at. Then build on that. Also, by the same token, find out what you're not good at and don't waste your time trying to perfect that.

— **Robert Armstrong**
Co-founder of the American Academy of Estate Planning Attorneys

I'm a real believer in dreams—you can't accomplish if you're not willing to dream. But I also think the worst thing that can happen is if you're only a dreamer. That's where the competitive piece comes into play—you must have the burning drive to finish everything that you set out to do. You must have a dream, and then you've got to finish the deal. It's no good for the ball to just get to the basket—to just get there. It has to go through the hoop.

— **Mick Aslin**
Chairman, Alterra Bank

One major aspect, definitely, is you've got to pick yourself up. But, you've got to pick everybody else up too. It's not just you… it's not about the business owner. It's not about the CEO or president. It is about everybody. If you fail badly here in this position, then you're going to fail—period. Then, everyone else in the company will follow suit and the company will fail. Respect plays a big role in this as does trust. You have to respect each other, you have to trust each other, you have to have fun and you have to enjoy the people you're around.

— **Bob Barnard**
President and Founder, Barnard Dunkelbert & Company

You are never comfortable. You have to learn to become increasingly comfortable with being uncomfortable. So, that's all I did. I sought out and listened to competent advisors—I've always tried to do that. I asked them to take my situation and see what perspectives I was missing. I had one tell me, "You now own this place AND you're the CEO of the business organization. Those are two entirely different roles. You have to realize the difference."

People have different life experiences. Certainly, people have different God-given talents, but the skill of leadership—like the skill of courage—is something that you either develop more of over your life or you don't. Courage and coping skills are things that we choose to develop or we don't choose to develop. That's my opinion. I see people work on improving and they grow. Because they grow, they inspire people around them. It's the art form of leading. Some people don't try to grow. They don't have any developmental process. They never set up a process in their adult life for being challenged, nor do those people want their thoughts, feelings or anything they do to be challenged. And they don't end up being a leader… why? Because they're not developing these skills.

— **Bryan Beaver**
Owner and CEO, CarterEnergy Corporation

One of first things people notice when they tour our plant is the big white board. The white board is called our squawk program. A squawk is a defect on an airplane. I happened to be flying one day and it occurred to me the term was on point to what we were trying to accomplish—improvement in the number of defects in our processes. It's a continuous improvement program that we put in place a number of years ago. Every employee has the ability and the responsibility to look for continuous improvements. In a nearly ten year period, we have had over 3,000 specifically identified improvements or changes to our processes or to our operations written on that white board. Some of those are changes to the changes. In other words, we found a better way to do something; then, maybe a year and a half or two years later, we found an even better way to do it.

So, our people have been involved in everything that I, personally, am not overseeing. People in the plant identify the improvement, it's tested and if it passes muster it goes on the white board. It's not my decision. That's the decision of what we call the squawk committee — a group of six people that changes every three months. They make those decisions. They can spend up to a thousand bucks without asking anybody. If it goes over that, then that's involving a little more capital expenditure; therefore, more people get involved. This has been a great thing for people. We have a 100% participation in that program. Everybody in the company has participated.

At various times, we have a point system that they've used to value how good a squawker suggestion was or how good an improvement it was. We also have a monetary reward on a quarterly basis.

But the monetary benefit is not why this has been so successful. You don't tie it to that kind of thing i.e. you save the company $10,000, you get $1,000. So many times you get into suggestion boxes — some people think that that's what this is. This is not a suggestion box deal. This is continuous improvement to the processes of the operations of the company. It can be anything. It causes people to think about the company — not just their job. They're thinking and saying, "How can I make Diamond better. I am interested in making Diamond a better place, as well as my own work environment better." That's a win-win for all of us.

— **Dick Seybolt**
CEO, Diamond Coach Corp.

PART II
PLANNING
Do You Know
Where You're Going?

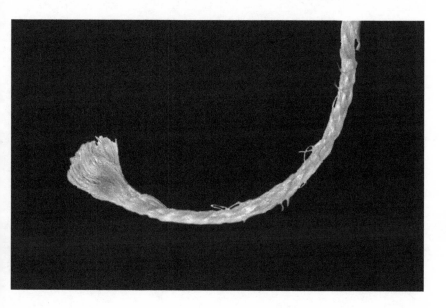

*"Plans are worthless,
but planning is everything."*
— General of the Army Dwight D. Eisenhower

Don't Start a Business; Instead Find a Market

Choosing the right business opportunity is one of the most important decisions you'll ever make. Lack of leadership, inadequate funding and poor financial controls can all cause a good business to go bad. But, the reverse isn't true. Having the right people and processes in place won't convert a poor opportunity into a great one. It's up to you to know the difference.

Unfortunately, most people don't. We start businesses for a variety of reasons... a desire to be our own boss as example, in a field where we have previous experience as an employee or practitioner... that is, as a technician, doing the thing the business does. Sometimes, we have a passion for a particular service or product, and we believe we can deliver it better than anyone else. Sometimes the motivation is geographically driven, such as wanting to own a quaint little bookstore on Cape Cod or dreaming of running our own five-star restaurant in the heart of New York City. Some do it because they want to be their own boss. And still others do it simply because they have an epiphany and it just seemed like the right thing to do at the time.

Regardless of what might have been the catalyst of the dream, the fact remains that the market has to be receptive or the business won't succeed. There has to be demand for your product or service and if there's not, that's something else you'll need to create. Many times there is an undiscovered demand. The demand for food is known. The demand for an iPhone was less apparent. It was created.

And this is where some good old fashioned research can come in handy.

Rather than starting a business, you want to first find a market... preferably one with potential or at least a market where future potential will occur. It might be a refinement of an existing market or the creation of an entirely new category. Regardless, you can then systematically create a plan for your business to excel by aligning the goals of your business with the needs of that market. Don't get me wrong...there is always an opportunity in any business. Just be sure the opportunity will take you where you want to go: Be sure it's big enough for you to achieve your goals. This point cannot be stated too strongly.

In the corporate world, research inspired Jack Welch to decide that General Electric would not pursue any business opportunity unless they could be #1 or #2 in the field. It had to be a very big opportunity for General Electric to make a commitment to it. All other business units were to be shed. New opportunities—in GE's case, the financial sector—were pursued because they could become #1 or #2 in that space. This strategy was not just about the capability of GE's management team — it was also about the opportunities the management team was willing to pursue. This was, perhaps, the most critical reason Welch's nearly 20 year tenure as CEO was marked with consistent, outstanding returns and stock price performance.

The late copywriting expert, Gary Halbert lived by this motto as well. In his seminars, he would offer attendees this challenge. They were told they owned a fast food restaurant and could choose any one thing they wanted that would give them a competitive advantage and achieve the fastest growth over all others. Some said they wanted a unique recipe. Others chose location, a unique menu, signage, staffing, the restaurant name and so forth. All failed the test.

At that point, Halbert revealed the true secret ingredient to success — he wanted a starving audience. So should you.

For the most part, business owners overlook the value of research in discovering opportunities within their chosen market. There are a multitude of ways to gather very precise data about your prospects, their attitudes about service providers, what makes them happy and what disappoints them. Do not overlook the important step of research in deciding what business you will enter or how to expand your current revenue streams.

Once you commit to this idea, it becomes easier to choose your opportunities wisely... the only question that remains is which market will be the right fit for you?

IT'S ALL IN THE NICHE

When working with our clients in our coaching groups, we talk about the importance of identifying niches. The analysis that goes with this decision is beyond the scope of this book, but I do want to just touch on some important things to remember:

The first repeats my earlier point: beyond knowing that the market exists, be sure your niche is big enough to support you and your goals. As example, providing marketing services to small start ups is most certainly a niche, but in that case, your business model will need to allow for the reality that many of your prospects will not have a large marketing budget. Taking on work for a client who cannot pay would require you to adjust your pricing or adjust the type of services you offer to make it work, thus potentially changing your business model.

That's not to say that it can't be done—just that you should have a clear understanding of how your chosen niche will compliment your goals.

The second point to remember is that your niche should be reachable. By this, I mean that it must be accessible to your firm and its marketing message given your financial resources. Obviously, the internet has drastically increased accessibility to the masses. But remember, you're not marketing to the masses . . . you're targeting a very specific niche. And it will be up to you to figure out how to get in front of that niche. Do you have a list of potential clients? Can you find them using online resources such as social networking platforms and online pay-per-click marketing? Will you have to rely on brick and mortar stores or distributors to get your product in front of your market? And how receptive is your market to new products and services?

These are questions business owners rarely ask, yet the answers are crucial to your success. Finding out now that accessibility is limited might not be the best news in the world, but it does allow you to make adjustments before you've invested extensive amounts of time and money to take your company in another direction. Adaptability, remember?

Your niche should also afford you an opportunity for growth, sometimes difficult to assess. Our society is very fad-oriented and we'll jump on the "next big thing" with great zeal and gusto, only to let it fade into oblivion when the next "next big thing" comes along.

Your business model can't just be based on what's hot right now—it has to be able to survive the ups and downs that go hand in hand with selling something to someone else. Look for long-term demand. In the 90's, collectible toys were quite the rage and many retailers made a killing selling hard-to-find toys to collectors. But it wasn't long before the manufacturers of those toys realized that the demand was bigger than their current supply. They could increase their bottom line simply by making more toys. They amped up production, flooded the market, and the small, collectible retailers suddenly found themselves without a market.

Blockbuster is another good example of a business model that was initially successful, although in this instance, it was more by lack of choice rather than design. There was a time when renting video cassettes and DVDs was THE thing to do... it was the fastest and easiest way to get your hands on new movies without investing twenty bucks for a DVD you may or may not like. The only caveat was that you had to physically go to a Blockbuster store to rent the movie and if you didn't return it in the allotted number of days, the fines would start to accumulate.

And for a while, that business model was acceptable. But then someone decided it could be done better and began doing research into alternative delivery systems.

All of a sudden, Netflix appeared. Not only could you rent DVDs from the comfort of your own home, but there were no penalties for keeping said DVDs a few extra days. In fact, Netflix got rid of late fees altogether and even introduced a service to let you stream some movies directly over the internet.

Could Blockbuster have offered the same services? Yes, and eventually they tried but by then, it was too little, too late. Netflix had already cornered the online video market and Blockbuster's once loyal client base had found a new home. The moral of this story is that no matter how good your original idea might be, the reality is that your market will probe your weaknesses, so your business needs to be out in front of the change, capable of changing and growing with it.

Of course, research isn't all there is to choosing a niche, but it's a good start and once you've identified the appropriate market, the planning can finally begin.

Turning Your Ideas into a Plan of Action

Now you have some certainty...research has confirmed the validity of your idea. You have decided it has the makings of a sustainable business, one that can withstand turbulence and the rigors of today's marketplace. The next step is to transform that idea into a plan of action. Like a great coach, you need a game plan. Surprisingly, this is a step that many business owners overlook.

And the reason is simple: who wants to spend time planning when there's money to be made out in the real world?

The truth is planning gives you the ability to check your facts and modify your assumptions . . . measure twice and cut once, as the saying goes. A good plan outlines the direction you're heading and helps you alter course when necessary without losing sight of your ultimate goal. And it's the first step in creating a business where there is 100% alignment between your plan and the daily actions taken by you and your team.

And trust me when I tell you that in a turbulent world you'll probably have to alter course more than once. Again, back to the sports analogy. You create a plan. Your opponent successfully reacts. Some coaches have built their entire reputation on their ability to make half-time adjustments. So should you.

There's just no way to know what the future holds and that means there's a good chance that you're going to have to make some changes along the way. Mick Aslin talked about the importance of flexibility during our interview, but only when that flexibility is tied to real, measurable results. "If your processes are in place," he says, "the results will occur."

The plan tells people what they are expected to do and outlines acceptable performance standards. Utilizing a results-based matrix, Aslin says, is what will define whether or not your plan was a success.

Now, what goes into your business plan will of course, depend upon a variety of factors, including your resources, your industry and the business concept itself. But that said, there are some issues concerning your business model that every business plan should address and it's those that we will address here.

BUSINESS MODEL OPTIONS

Many of you are already in business. If not, first and foremost, you need to establish your business entity. This goes far beyond simply choosing between a sole proprietorship and incorporating. If you are starting from scratch, factor in asset protection and tax liability issues when making your entity formation decisions.

In addition to deciding what type of legal entity you'll own, you should also consider the ways that your business will generate income. Put simply: exactly what will you do to earn money? There are several options and you need to be clear about where you fit, because some offer more opportunity than others.

In the professional service industry for example, the classic model is receiving money in exchange for time and skill. A sole-practicing dentist and his hygienists trade their time and skill for patients paying them money for the service. Whether paid by the hour, the project or job, the same is true of many small law firms, chiropractors, and other small business owners.

Add another professional to help provide the service, and you move to a model of getting money for other people's time. As the owner you get a portion of the money generated by your associate's time with customers, clients or patients. This provides you—the owner—with leverage, because not only are you earning for your personal contributions to the company, but you're now also generating income from someone else's efforts. Of course, this model requires capital to cover the additional overhead, at least for a period of time. But it does, in essence, add another professional to your staff, thus another source of revenue for your business.

If the business grew more, the next model would involve receiving money for other people's time AND money. The most common example of this model is a partnership where your business receives income not just from the efforts of the new associate but also benefits from the associate's monetary investment into the company or firm as a partner. This investment represents capital that your business can now use to generate additional income or continue on its path of growth and expansion. At this level, you're making more money and if planned correctly, working fewer hours. In other words you are receiving money and time for other people's money and time.

Of course, this is just the tip of the iceberg. There are online business model options as well—strategic alliances, affiliate marketing, advertising and subscription-based programs to name just a few, and if you're selling tangible products... well, that introduces a new collection of business models as well.

Ultimately, only you can decide which model will fit best and yes, you may decide to add and delete models as your business evolves or have different models underneath your business umbrella. Regardless of which model you choose, you should be aware of each and every source of revenue available to your company at any time, and all of these options should be reflected in your plan.

This will require you to create projections and engage in forecasting—to look beyond the next year or two and decide where you'd like your company to go. To do this, you'll need a planning model to help you address the basic components, so let's start there. Don't forget to conduct these steps with turbulence in mind. It's stormy out there.

THE STRATEGIC ALIGNMENT MODEL — PART 1: WHERE ARE WE GOING?

W hen Alice asked the Cheshire Cat, "Would you tell me, please, which way I ought to go from here?" The Cat replied, "That depends a good deal on where you want to get to."

"I don't much care where..." Alice responded.

"Then it doesn't matter which way you go," said the Cat.

"...as long as I get *somewhere*," she countered.

"Oh, you're sure to do that," said the Cat, "if only you walk long enough."

Without a solid plan, your company is just like Alice — wandering aimlessly in Wonderland, unsure of which path she should take next, thinking any path will do. Now in a strong market, you might get away with winging it for a while, and perhaps even enjoy some profitable, albeit chaotic success.

And with all the available material about "strategic planning," you might wonder why I would devote a significant amount of time to it in this book. The reason is because I believe conventional strategic planning has it all wrong. Too many plans end up as theoretical exercises, delivered in a large binder that go on a shelf, never to be opened again.

The strategic planning process we use on the other hand, is intentional, part of an overall performance management system. It is a working tool that aligns what you aspire to achieve with your business to ground level actions and behaviors that lead to desired results. And it's easy to use. It encourages speed of implementation, includes feedback systems and ensures accountability. Most importantly, it dramatically improves the likelihood of better bottom line results.

Obviously, having that kind of edge becomes even more important in a turbulent market. The choice of course, is yours but if you decide not to have a planning system, then I suggest you don't get too comfortable in that office. Because without a plan, your business will underachieve. And in today's competitive marketplace, the underachievers don't last long.

Now, to get us started, we've divided the planning section into two broad categories. In this Part 1, we'll ask the big questions—Where are we? And, where are we going? In Part 2, we'll show you how to find the answers.

WHAT IS THE CURRENT SITUATION?

The first step in any journey is to determine where we are . . . the "as is" of your business. This includes not just the basics such as financial strength and product demand, but also an analysis of what your company brings to the table. You need to know what you do well and what you don't, as well as what challenges you'll need to overcome and what opportunities lie ahead. This is what's known as an environmental assessment. Now, you've probably heard this referred to as a SWOT Analysis, but I prefer SCOT—Strengths, Challenges, Opportunities and Threats. Strengths and Challenges (or Weaknesses) are internal factors to consider. Opportunities and Threats are external factors that could impact your business.

A SCOT analysis is designed to show you where you are now and, in the process, help you identify both hidden and known issues—internally and externally — that will affect how you move forward. The SCOT analysis is traditionally done using a simple four-quadrant matrix that allows you to see your bigger picture and identify the areas that you can build upon or those that need attention.

Strengths	Challenges
Internal skills, talents and factors that can be used as a foundation for growth.	Internal issues and concerns that can hinder growth.
Opportunities	**Threats**
External events or conditions that will help you reach your goals.	External issues and concerns that can prevent or hinder you from reaching your goals.

And here's how you use it:

Strengths

Examples of strengths could be the patent you own on a particular product, your current competitive advantage (it's never service or quality and should not be pricing), the location of your establishment, brand recognition and the like.

To determine your strengths, you'll want to ask the following questions:

1. What identifiable advantages do you currently have over the competition?
2. Why should customers buy from you instead of someone else?
3. How is your fulfillment, product or service distinguishable from all others?
4. What has made your company successful so far?
5. What talents and skills does your management team bring to the table?
6. What are your company's strongest points?

The test is not how you would answer these questions—it's how an independent, third party would answer them. One thing to note: Your competitive advantage or strengths are not traits or characteristics that could be listed by your competitors as well. For example, if all your competitors have global capabilities, then the fact that your company has it isn't a strength… it's just the nature of your particular niche.

And since we're talking about what is and isn't a strength, great quality and great service are not competitive advantages. In today's highly competitive and turbulent marketplace, offering great quality and great service are a given. They are admission tickets. Even Wal-Mart, the king-pin of a low cost provider, has greeters waiting at points of entry to their stores and offer acceptable quality for the price point — at least in the opinions of the millions who shop there.

Challenges

These are those insidious little creatures that gestate within any organization . . . creeping up on you, often unrecognized until the damage is well underway. Example challenges could include high overhead relative to sales (i.e. margin issues), a lack of reliable vendors, poor physical location, inexperienced staff or high staff turnover, poor brand recognition, poor service reputation… you get the idea.

To determine your challenges, ask the following questions:

1.   Which products or services in your market are overly competitive?
2.   Which products have licensing, patent or other production or distribution issues?
3.   What could you do better?
4.   What areas have the lowest sales?
5.   What areas have the lowest repeat sales?
6.   What generates the most client complaints?
7.   Where are the bottlenecks and what causes them?

It's important that you be painfully honest during this process. Give these questions some thought. Then think about how you can either minimize the effect of these weaknesses or perhaps put an end to them altogether.

For example, if a lack of quality distributors is a problem, then creating a plan to identify and negotiate an agreement with new distributors might be your best course of action. Here's a tip: Do not shy away from identifying challenges. On the reverse side of the challenge coin may lay an opportunity.

Opportunities

How do you leverage your strengths to maximize opportunities or find opportunity embedded in a challenge or threat? Opportunities are external factors that benefit you and your business…events or circumstances that you can build upon to grow your company. Examples include new technologies, new distribution or marketing channels, new processes, new products and services and trends or developments that create a new customer need.

To pinpoint your opportunities, you'll need to look at your market and ask the following questions:

1. How do the latest technologies affect your products and services?
2. How do the latest technologies affect your customers' needs?
3. What opportunities can be created by utilizing your strengths?
4. What opportunities can be created by eliminating a challenge?
5. What affect do current trends and social patterns have on your business?
6. What else is our customer buying from someone else that we can sell him?
7. What's changing in our customers' purchasing patterns that remains undiscovered by the marketplace?
8. How can we create a "category of one" doing or offering something no one else can offer?

When listing opportunities, be extremely open and optimistic. Remember, all the great leaders didn't get to the top by thinking safe and conservatively. Yes, you'll definitely want to identify some opportunities that you can capitalize on in a relatively short period of time, but that doesn't mean you should throw everything else out. Instead, think outside of the box… hell, throw away the box and see what happens. It's not analytical thinking and conservative reason that will get you where you want to go… its innovation.

Now, this doesn't mean that you're committing to every wild idea that might pop into your head. As American Academy of Estate Planning Attorneys' co-founder Sanford M. Fisch points out, one of the most important things you'll do as a CEO is learn when to say "no."

"All business owners are bombarded with opportunities," he said. "If you can't say no, then you're going to be like the old Pac-Man game where you're just turning in one direction and then another . . . never making any progress. You'll always be distracted by the shiny new object and these days, there are more shiny new objects than ever before. That's how you assess the opportunity. Is it in line with my ultimate goal? If not, then you have to say maybe later, but not now." And that brings us back to the importance of a clear vision. It creates an automatic opportunity filter, helping you know when to say, "Yes," and more importantly, when to say "No."

Threats

Threats are external factors that can hinder your business, and perhaps even kill it. Examples include new technologies, new regulations, new taxes or fees, price increases, new competition and of course, concerns stemming from economic and/or environmental issues.

Earlier, I mentioned the legal profession's resistance to the digital revolution and I'll use that example again here. When analyzing threats, a smart attorney would consider how online competition might affect his firm's bottom line so that he could make an informed decision about how best to proceed. Unfortunately, most attorneys aren't making that analysis and if that doesn't change, we'll see a number of those law firms disappear.

To identify your threats, look at the world around you and ask the following questions:

1. How do the latest technologies affect your products and services?
2. How do the latest technologies affect your customers' needs?
3. How is the current economic situation affecting your company?
4. How might new regulations impact your business?
5. How will you be able to compete if a well capitalized company declares a price war?
6. What other factors or issues would cause serious harm to your company?

While the line of thinking here isn't optimistic, it is important to remain outside the box when listing your threats. Being able to identify possible threats, even if they haven't occurred yet, enables you to think about how you would respond if and when they do. It's called developing Plan B, C and D.

Following our SCOT analysis, we must recognize an important fact. Planning isn't foolproof and in fact, most of them technically fail.

George Foreman, the famous heavyweight boxing champ has been heard to say, "Everyone has a plan until they get hit in the nose." Likewise, military leaders have observed that even perfect plans tend to go awry when the first shot is fired. Spiritual advisors join in by reminding us, "You know how to make God mad? Tell him your plan."

But it's not really the process of planning that brings failure—it's the point of view from which the plan is formed. Plans tend to assume the best circumstances and are often made from a very optimistic state of mind. Or, they are statements of wishful thinking with no execution backbone. When we're planning a trip for instance, we factor in the time and expenses directly related to the event, but we don't typically allow for things like car trouble, lost credit cards or flight delays. Even the average household budget— perhaps the simplest example of a "plan"—frequently fails because it doesn't allow for the unexpected. And in a world where change—even turbulence — is the only true constant, encountering the unexpected is the one thing you can expect.

So, while we're going to start from the optimistic view of your vision, we're also going to ensure that your planning process devotes some time to anticipating the unknown. Strategic planning is more than analyzing the strengths and weaknesses of your products and services and those of your competitors, more than long-range planning and business trends and more than reviewing and analyzing numbers to project the future. It is a pro-active, holistic approach to building a business that creates your future instead of simply reacting to current business trends.

What that means is that, for most business owners and CEOs, you can forget about strategic planning as it's described in the MBA textbooks. That approach is nothing more than a waste of a good binder… a 200-page tome that serves as a dust cover for the wood shelf it occupies. Actually, the binder is worth more.

Instead, a Strategic Alignment Plan ("SAP") is an action plan — one with a clear vision and purpose, nimble and with durability and rapid-change capability to withstand hurricane-like forces of the unexpected. It is applied with energy and speed, with built-in accountability and it contains a commitment to execution. Its objective is to ensure you thrive, not merely survive. I say thrive because the idea is to prosper—big time—not just get by. Survival doesn't captivate me… How about you?

A SAP is a working instrument, a tool you use every day, not a document archived for the ages—it should help you get to where you want to go, not simply remind you of an idea you once had.

Here's a case in point. As I write this I am sitting on a Southwest Airlines flight about to depart from Philadelphia. We'll stop over in St. Louis, and then fly on to Oklahoma City. Rest assured the pilot has a plan that includes more than just the optimistic flight plan he files with air traffic control. That plan might be the basis for how the airline estimates our arrival time and the flight path from Point A to B; but the pilots and computers constantly make adjustments along the way to accommodate the unexpected. Maybe they have to divert because of thunderstorms. Maybe an engine fails or a landing gear won't deploy or their navigation system malfunctions. Regardless of how big or how small the variation might be, those pilots are trained to always have a Plan B to anticipate the unexpected.

Captain C.B. Sullenberger, the now famous United Airlines captain certainly demonstrated the power of having a Plan B when he executed a successful landing of his plane in the Hudson River following engine failure—the result of a freak encounter with birds.

Hello, unexpected . . . hello turbulence… literally.

Captain Sullenberger couldn't have made that landing without some Plan B preparation, not to mention courage, confidence and the wisdom that comes from experience. His goal was to land the plane on its rear wheels or on its belly. That had to be top priority. Next, was to be sure the plane did not flip. Where he landed was less important than how he landed. It was critical to preserve the safety of its passengers—he just had to utilize some creative thinking to make that happen.

The point is pilots utilize flight plans as working tools, ones created to manage the variables to assure a successful landing at the intended destination, at the estimated time of arrival. CEOs, business owners, entrepreneurs and managers would do well to think like "Sully" and to have their strategic plan do the same.

And here's the big bonus you receive for engaging the planning process. You'll grow to understand your business better. Having to think about revenue streams, client acquisition cost, revenue per employee, line by line operating expenses, employee productivity, the cost of creating more top line revenue and a multitude of other issues will put you in touch with reality and prepare you for the efforts required to achieve your financial goals. There's much more to this than simply announcing, "We're going to grow our sales by 20% this year." In fact, that's not planning. That's guessing.

You have to be much better than that. Turbulence demands it.

What follows is the formula we use in our coaching programs to help our participants develop their plan. There are of course, many ways to identify the elements of a strategic plan. Michael Gerber starts with a Primary Aim. The U.S. military starts with defining the mission. Some start by creating a vision.

The key is to answer the Why, What, How, Who, and When questions. Do that and you will have a plan for turbulent times, and if you follow our guidelines, you will have alignment from the top of your organization to the bottom. Everyone on your team will know where you are headed, your expectations, their role in this grand scheme you've concocted and what success looks like.

For us, those questions can best be answered by having these elements as part of the planning process:

- Vision – A statement of where or who you want your company to be three-five years from now; what your firm will contribute to your life and why you are on this journey;
- Mission – What will be done during the next year to move your company closer to achieving your vision;
- Core Values – The attitudes and behaviors your firm and it's team members make to one another and to your constituencies;
- Critical Success Factors – Structures, systems and capabilities we must have in place to achieve our Mission;
- Strategic Objectives or Goals – What must happen for us to achieve our Critical Success Factors;
- Action Steps – Specific statements of who does what and by when to achieve our Goals, and;

- Alignment Processes – A method of ensuring these processes are implemented throughout your organization.

Now, having thoroughly convinced you of the presence of permanent turbulence and the elements of a great plan, let's go back to an optimistic viewpoint and examine the first piece of your planning puzzle.

CREATING A VISION — IF IT'S CLOUDY IN THE PULPIT IT'S FOGGY IN THE PEW

It's often been said, "We'd better pay attention to the future, because that's where we're going to spend the rest of our lives." The foundation for success in any business is a clear picture of where that business is going, and what you want the end result to be (even though there's technically no "end"). So, if it's "cloudy" in your mind, it will be "foggy" to those you lead… and these are the people you will need to help you achieve your dream.

Having a clear vision statement then, is crucial to your success.

Your vision statement describes where you want your company to be in the future, its contribution to your personal life and why you chose this path and this vehicle. It is a vivid, mental picture of that future and unlike the rest of your reality, it is the one time I encourage you to imagine only the biggest, brightest and best future possible. This is your time to commit to the proposition that we can either create the life we wish to live or defer to fate and take what comes our way.

Stephen Covey's *Seven Habits of Highly Effective People* reminds us that all planning begins with the end in mind. Michael Gerber's process calls it the Primary Aim. Regardless of how you label it, the vision step is the process of thinking about and envisioning the professional and personal future to which you aspire, and the growth required to achieve that future state.

To illustrate the importance of "seeing the end," Guardian Equity Group's President, John Dudeck tells the story of participating in a board-breaking exercise with his son. The instructor shows John how to punch his fist through the board and then asks him to take his turn.

"So, I rear back with all my might," he says, "and smashed my fist and my knuckles against the board. It hurt like hell and the board didn't break." The instructor then asked John where he had focused when he hit the board. John pointed to the board.

"Wrong focus," the instructor said. Instead, the instructor told John that he should have focused on the *space beyond and behind the board*—the space that represented the possibilities of where John wanted his fist to be. He asked John to get up and try it again… and he did.

John smashed the board on the first try.

"I'll never forget the lesson because it was so great in many respects," he said. "I had to be thinking about my follow through. I couldn't be thinking about the obstacle in front of me—I had to be thinking about the space beyond the board which, for me, represented the possibilities."

FUTURECASTING

This concept of seeing the end result is also often referred to as "futurecasting"—that is, imagining (instead of predicting) a future that encompasses the ideas and values you desire your project to have. In essence, you need to see the future you prefer instead of just a future that's possible. And that brings us to the heart of the vision creation process: what exactly does your Future Picture look like?

Interestingly, this is not always an easy question to answer.

For many CEOs and entrepreneurs, they simply haven't gotten that far in the planning process. They just start working, hoping someone will follow and that things work out for the best. For example, an attorney might know that he wants to run his own firm, but he may have no idea as to how that firm will look five or ten years from now. Will he still want to spend his days in the courtroom or would he prefer to one day take off his technician's hat and move into a leadership position instead? In the meantime, he just starts doing the technician's work, wondering where it might lead.

Likewise, a web design company might understand the importance of staying on top of all the latest technology and trends, but it's how they could use those new technologies and trends to develop new products and services that will ensure their future success.

It's critical to see the difference between creating your future by design versus letting it happen by default. One holds the potential to engineer amazing success while the other almost guarantees that you'll always be scrambling to "just get by." I refer to this as living life by the "pinball effect." You can choose to either be the one standing up, controlling the levers or you can resign yourself to being the pinball and just going wherever you happen to be pushed. The fact that you're reading this tells me which one you'd likely choose.

Chance, hope and other vagaries of the marketplace or your mind should not be allowed to be members of your firm nor a participant in your future. Do not let them control your business destiny or your life.

So, let's turn this brain-storming session to your business and ask a few questions. Your goal here is to think big, and you can do that by answering the following questions:

- Where do you see your business in three years? *Why three? Because it's easier to keep a three year vision action-oriented. Less pie in the sky.*
- What professional goals would you like your company to meet?
- How much money will you want your business to generate for you and your family?
- How many employees would you like to have on staff?
- What services or products do you want to offer? What needs or desires do those services and products meet?
- What kind of personal lifestyle does your business allow you to have?
- How often do you travel? Is it strictly business or does your company afford you the ability to take time off and see the world?
- Who takes care of the day-to-day operations? Can your business run efficiently when you're not in the office?
- Is your vision in line with your personal values and lifestyle?

You get the idea. These questions are asked in present tense, meaning that the mission statement talks about your company as it is NOW.

Your vision is the foundation that your business is built upon and it should be something that both you and your employees value … exciting and bold, inspiring everyone in the company to reach for it. It should be challenging, yet realistic enough that you can imagine attaining it. It also needs to be clear and vivid, defining the path you need to take to turn that vision into reality. Remember the stonecutter story from Chapter 2? This is where you define your "cathedral" and unite your stonecutters with a shared vision.

In short, your Vision should be grand, the driving force behind your business and the next component of your plan—your Mission.

VISION VS. MISSION

Now, since we're on the subject of defining your vision, let's also take just a minute to talk about your mission.

Interestingly, CEOs are much more familiar with the idea of writing a mission statement than they are defining a vision, despite the fact that your mission doesn't exist without a vision to ignite it.

Where vision statements articulate a future picture of what you aspire to achieve with your business, a mission statement addresses what you do to reach your goals and continue to meet your obligations. In today's turbulent times I am hesitant to think in five or ten year planning horizons. Instead, we prefer our coaching and consulting clients to consider their Vision over a three year time horizon, and their mission statement on what they will do over the next 12 months to achieve their three year Vision. I call it my 3:1 planning formula. Now, there's no hard and fast rule on this. For you, a 5:2 formula may be better, thinking of your Vision over five years and your mission actions over a two year period. My point is to give careful thought as to how a time frame influences your plan.

I offer two examples. If you think things will always be the same and build a company using yesterday's assumptions to pursue present and future opportunities, you may create irrelevant capability. Think of the U.S. military. They have the ultimate challenge. Only time will tell, but I'm guessing the U.S. Army's amazing M1 Abrams tank, the most amazing ground-based war machine ever created, will play a reduced role in future high-tech warfare. I'm not saying the Abrams is irrelevant. I'm simply raising a question. Not all wars will be fought in a desert. Yet we have billions of dollars tied up in Abrams inventory. Will that inventory play a vital role in defending our nation in the future? I have no idea. If not, think of the sunk costs embedded in that powerful, yet idle, capability. On the other hand, project demand too far into the future, or base demand estimates on an agenda that's irrelevant to the task of selling your product or service, and you develop a product or service no one wants. I cite General Motor's Volt as the poster-child of this point. It may be the right car for the future but is it the right car at this time? Is it a car people will buy now? Perhaps demand will increase for an alternative energy car that runs on electricity created from fossil fuel and coal-fired generating plants. In the meantime, people are shunning government handouts in the form of tax credits, still refusing to buy it.

The purpose of the mission statement is to define what has to be done within the next 12 months to move you quantifiably closer to your vision using the opportunities, tools and resources you have at this moment. This is where you outline your most immediate strategies—the "what" you will do. Again, in our work with clients helping them develop their plans, the mission statement takes the three year view of their vision and breaks it down into strategies and milestones achievable within one year.

Having both a big-picture, future-based vision statement and a present-focused mission statement ensures that everyone in your company understands both—where it is the company wants to go as well as the strategies that must be implemented to get there... and this is important.

The human spirit is naturally disposed to believe in something bigger than itself and it is this notion that forms the foundation for your vision statement. Your employees will work better and harder and faster when they truly believe in and value the work they're doing, a topic we're going to cover in-depth a little later on. But they also need the mission statement to define the more immediate strategies and illustrate the plan they'll be using to build that cathedral.

ADDING IN YOUR CORE VALUES

Okay, so we know your mission statement acknowledges where you are now while your vision statement covers how you see the future. Now you need to create a set of values that will define the standards and guidelines you'll follow to get from here to there.

Your value statement ensures that your company isn't just on track, but on a track that corresponds with the beliefs and values you hold most dear. Why is that so important? Because these values will form the culture within your company... and we all know that culture has a direct effect on individual behaviors.

In fact, your corporate values and the culture they create will define how your company does business. It will determine how your employees interact and perform, how your clients are treated and how the actions of your company and its people are measured. Someone who works in a way that is counter-intuitive to this culture will "stand out" to others within the company and likewise, won't be very happy with their working environment.

And this is exactly why having a statement of core values is so important. Identifying and establishing a clear set of values allows you to hire personnel with congruent beliefs… and the more your corporate values mesh with that of your employees, the more balanced and "in sync" your company will be.

Think about it: where would you be more productive—in a company with similar values and work ethics or in an environment with situational values. Again, be clear . . . your company has a set of values. Who set them? If not, do you know what they are? Does it contribute or detract from your vision?

Because that's really what we're talking about when we say "corporate culture"… it's the personality of your company and that collective personality is made up of all the individual personalities and value systems working within. That's why some people seem to "fit" while others just don't.

It makes sense then to create your core values statement from the bottom-up rather than top-down. It's this mindset that made retail giant Zappos so incredibly successful. Using a question-and-answer system that allowed CEO Tony Hsieh to align the corporate culture with the values of its employees, Zappos came up with the following ten core values:

- Deliver WOW through service
- Embrace and drive change
- Create fun and a little weirdness
- Be adventurous, creative and open-minded
- Pursue growth and learning
- Build open and honest relationships with communication
- Build a positive team and family spirit
- Do more with less
- Be passionate and determined
- Be humble

Kind of sets the tone for the day, doesn't it?

These ten values shape how the employees work within the company. They define the Zappos brand and provide a blueprint for the processes and strategies used to promote that brand. They also ensure that each and every employee comes to work with a sense of purpose and responsibility to the bigger, corporate picture... and you see the results.

Now, what's really interesting about these ten values is that they very closely model Hsieh's list of personal core values, and it's this alignment that allowed Zappos to create the successful empire we know today. You can use Hsieh's model to create core values for your company by downloading the free Mountains and Valleys exercise from CultureSync (www.culturesync.net/happiness). This exercise walks you through the process of identifying your personal values by measuring the high and low points of your life, and then using those as a foundation to create your corporate culture.

Here are the core values for our firm:

- Demonstrate the Golden Rule;
- Go beyond lagniappe service;
- Be a promise keeper;
- Get better every day; and,
- Show passion for what you do and share it

I strongly recommend you complete this exercise yourself and then share it with your key personnel . . . in fact, share it with all of your personnel if it's reasonable to do so. The more input you have from your team, the more rewarding and productive your corporate culture will be.

IDENTIFYING CRITICAL SUCCESS FACTORS

Now that you know your vision, mission and core values, the next step is to identify those things that are both necessary and sufficient to achieve the mission. Let's call them critical success factors ("CSFs"). Think of them as ingredients in a business success recipe. Since your mission operates on a one year time frame, so do the critical success factors that support your mission. They will also be consistent with and provide guidelines for the next step in our planning process, setting goals and developing actions steps.

Critical success factors are, by design generally more specific than the mission, yet not as specific as goals. When working with our coaching and consulting clients, I want them to be clear about their CSFs, those structures, systems and capabilities that must be present to achieve your mission. And while there's no set rule on how many you should have, four to eight critical success factors is a good number to start with.

Our clients have listed these, among others, as critical success factors:

- Multiple revenue streams;
- A hiring system that staffs for strengths, fast learning and a "get things done" attitude;
- Behaviors reflect our core values;
- Accurate measurement and timely reporting of actions and outcomes;
- Fully integrated, effective lead generation systems;
- Outstanding conversion percentages;
- Simple, accurate, speedy, one-way fulfillment systems that exceed expectations;
- Timely, accurate feedback systems—financial and client; observed or reported.

As you can see, critical success factors differ from core values but like core values, they can serve as the blueprint for your day-to-day operations and offer a daily reminder to a business owner or CEO of what should be the object of their highest attention.

There are many other CSFs you may want to choose. It's important to determine what they are for your business by modeling them to fit your mission and your vision. A CSF could be to introduce one new product each year or expand your existing operations into new geographic locations or markets. You don't have to know which locations or markets just yet, nor do you have to choose between geographic expansion and a broader product base... in fact, you might want to do both. And that's the great thing about critical success factors—you're not limited to just one.

You could also add a growing amount of repeat business, multiple branding strategies and cutting the cost of production each year to that list. Again, they will differ for each firm and that's a good thing... because no two companies are exactly alike.

Regardless of how many you have, all of your CSFs should be crucial ingredients to your business—meaning that in order for you to accomplish your mission, these CSFs absolutely have to be in place.

This is why simply having a mission of increasing your profits isn't enough—you have to know the architecture for making that happen is in place. Coming up we will show you how to define how you'll create that increase in profitability by laying out the specific steps that you'll need to take to achieve your vision.

Critical success factors can relate to any aspect of your business, including education, customer service, quality control, training, personnel, research and development, marketing and of course, finances, but don't worry... this process is easier than you might think.

Vision, mission, core values and critical success factors should be analyzed from top down and from bottom up, making adjustments as required until there is perfect alignment. Notice critical success factors are not goals. There are no numbers associated with critical success factors. They are ingredients; structures, systems and capabilities that have to be present within your organization. Think chocolate chip cookies. You can't make them without the chocolate chips.

After you have determined your firm's vision, mission, core values and critical success factors you can start thinking about bringing other team members into the process. This is the critical part of the Strategic Alignment Plan I mentioned earlier. It's where actions and alignment becomes part of the equation. This is the point where we start looking at Strategic Objectives or the goal setting process. When team members are creating goals and taking actions that are consistent with your vision, mission, core values and critical success factors there will be alignment within your organization that was unknown before.

Now it's time to start drilling down into specifics, getting our hands dirty in the planning process.

THE STRATEGIC
ALIGNMENT MODEL —
PART 2: SETTING
THINGS IN MOTION

With your foundation built—vision, mission, core values and critical success factors in place, you now need to define a few parameters that will guide you through the balance of developing your Strategic Alignment Plan and make it become operational. These parameters are what will get you and your team from "here" to "there" and help you do it in a way that meshes with those all-important beliefs and values.

To do this, we'll start just like we did in the first part of the strategic action planning model—with the big picture, and then work our way down to the details.

THE HEART – THE ACTION AND ALIGNMENT PLAN

So far, we've started the process of creating a strategic blueprint for your overall success during turbulent times. Now it's time to start thinking about how you'll actually get there. That's why the next step in your Strategic Alignment adventure is for you and your team to create your Action and Alignment Plan. Here we set goals, consider obstacles, create timelines and assign responsibilities and create alignment by utilizing this process throughout our organization. Many business owners and CEOs feel fairly comfortable with the first few steps. Most miss the last step. It is a critical factor in thriving during severe turbulence.

One caveat: do not assume everyone on your team is as committed to goal setting as you may be. In fact, you may not be a goal setter. Maybe it's a matter of semantics and formalities. I've worked with people who say they are not goal setters, yet they achieve goals. They are instinctive achievers who relentlessly pursue goals. They may not call them goals but they like to see ever-increasing tangible results. Regardless of what you like to call it, I encourage you to understand the process and utilize the benefits of goal setting to create a culture that achieves results. You, or someone you select, may have to coach and train for it to permeate your organization.

Also understand that while no one likes to talk about it, you have to assume there will be those on your team who will sabotage your efforts. They exist in virtually every organization. It might be subtle, overt, behind your back or outrageous and in your face. In any event, you need to plan for sabotage. Then implement your action and alignment plan and manage based on commitments made. Follow up for accountability and you will quickly identify those not on the same page. Then eliminate them.

Setting objectives—goal-setting—is a necessity in the business world, if not life in general. At the end of the day, it's the only way we can establish accountabilities. If you say you want to increase your profits, most of us consider that a goal. Perhaps, you would like to book seven new clients this month? That could be a goal as well. Want to exercise more, lose weight, buy a new house or spend more time with your family? Those could be goals too… albeit goals of a personal kind. But as stated, these are only a wish. Something you hope for and dream about doing someday. They are not real goals until they have specificity and accountability attached. Dreams die in the absence of specificity and accountability just as engines die without fuel.

As proof of that fact, the participants who make the most progress in our coaching groups are those who are most willing to be vulnerable by asking questions, who are teachable and who are willing to be accountable to the coaches and the group. Reread that sentence. It's one of the most important sentences in this book.

In my coaching experience here's how most people approach goal setting: You set a goal and then you figure out how to get from A to B.

Too often people—yes, business owners and CEOs—forget that last step. Setting a goal is almost a waste of time absent a plan of actions required to achieve it. In fact, the action phase is where the much heralded concept of execution lives.

Goal setting sounds simple in theory yet for many, reaching those goals has proved to be consistently difficult. Here are two very common reasons for this difficulty:

The first is that the goal doesn't really provide direction. While "increasing sales" might sound like a good, broad goal for example, it doesn't really tell your sales staff how to reach that particular milestone. Direction is everything if you want to achieve that goal and still adhere to your vision and values. No specificity. No accountability.

You've just spent some considerable amount of time and energy defining the vision, mission, core values and critical success factors that you want your company to achieve and live by—now apply that same clarity and enthusiasm to the goal setting process.

Most of us have heard of setting SMART goals. The SMART goal-setting method—specific, measurable, achievable, relevant (some say "realistic") and time-based—is a good place to start, but don't forget to make your goals even more meaningful by adding accountability and other standards to the mix; such as activities consistent with your core values.

What if, for example, you decided that your goals must be empowering to the employees working to reach them . . . can you imagine what that kind of goal-setting would do for company morale?

Or suppose that goals must require the employee to broaden their horizons in some way or that it must meet certain criteria to be deemed challenging...how much more would your company accomplish if all its goals encouraged your employees to push the envelope and test their own limits?

Maybe you want your goals to be environmentally responsible or responsive to issues in your community... just as you can insist that your goals are measurable and realistic, you can also ensure that they're group oriented or based on solid research to be accepted.

They're your goals, so think big and reach for the stars. Yes, generic goals such as increasing sales can still be an element of the process—you just need to give it some direction by defining how that goal can be reached with specificity and accountability. If it cannot be measured and tracked, it's not specific enough.

The second reason that goal-setting often fails is that the goal itself doesn't fit with your current structure or environment. In effect, it's not realistic. It's unreasonable, for example to set a goal to increase sales by 35% if you're not going to give your sales staff any new tools or resources to work with . . . especially when you're operating in such a turbulent market. This type of goal indirectly suggests that the sales staff isn't doing their job as well as they could, a subliminal message that can wreak havoc on company morale.

Be careful your goals do not pit your team against each other, encouraging cut-throat tactics to avoid any potential punishment that might result from not reaching the lofty goals you've set. Clearly, this is no way to run a business and you can bet that any growth you do see will be short-lived.

Instead, think about how you might increase those sales and then set quotas or milestones that are realistic to each division or employee. Is there a new product or service you can offer? Is there an obstacle that has kept your company from reaching those milestones in the past?

Of course, one way to get input about these questions is to ask the people who would be responsible for meeting those goals. Anticipate some of them will resist ever-increasing sales goals, but their buy-in is important. They'll know exactly what's realistic and what's not and they'll be more than capable of telling you what needs to happen to make that situation change. Let them have some input in setting organizational goals and even more when setting goals for which they will be accountable.

Your job is to listen… and then create some mutually agreed-upon goals that move you toward achieving your mission, thus moving you closer to actualizing the vision of what your firm will be. All of this can be done in a positive manner, one that motivates your team at the same time. Involve your employees in the growth process and you'll see success. You'll experience alignment and better results. Engage in an autocratic top-down management style that encourages an "every-man-for-himself" mentality, and you'll fail miserably every single time.

When working with your team you should treat goals as commitments and be sure you communicate the expectation that when team members agree to a goal, they are making a commitment to achieve it. Constantly reinforce this notion of their commitments when discussing progress.

Once goals, responsibilities and timelines are set, it is time for execution.

THE DIFFERENCE MAKER – THE 30-DAY ACTION PLAN

The 30-Day action plan is what breathes life into your vision and mission. It is your vision and mission statements in action…getting things done… execution. Operating in tandem with your core values and critical success factors, each team member develops specific actions—clear and achievable milestones—to be taken over the next 30 days. When implemented, the 30 Day Action Plan will start you and your organization on the journey toward your desired destination. After goals are created and actions identified, we need to be sure we have alignment throughout our organization and accountability for performance.

Actions are the logical step in the journey toward achieving goals. Which actions you choose will of course, depend upon your goals, your market, your niche and yes, the strengths, weaknesses, opportunities and threats that are unique to your team and your company.

Obviously the actions you choose should be those most likely to achieve a goal. When setting goals and corresponding action steps be sure they are consistent with your critical success factors. They help everyone stay aimed at True North.

For example, you may be behind the times when it comes to utilizing technology and you set a goal of upgrading those capabilities. You deem it critical to your success. If so, a component of your strategy is strengthening this part of your business. Maybe your website needs to be revamped… perhaps you need to take advantage of online advertising resources or you need a full-blown internet store in order to compete… all of these ideas could be strategies that get you closer to marking this weakness off your list.

This doesn't mean that you'll be able to eliminate every weakness just as you won't take advantage of every opportunity—but that's the whole point of the planning process… it allows you to decide how you want to move forward.

And then once your decision is made it's time to take action, knowing that as you move forward, you'll encounter distractions along the way.

Author, speaker and business consultant, Greg Hunt illustrated this point when he reminded me of the Kentucky Fried Chicken story. Not so long ago, KFC decided to branch out into other food products. Rather than see a big increase in their bottom line, they found their business to be floundering. The powers that be realized they were doing too much and decided to focus on what they did best.... And "We Do Chicken Right" was born.

"I feel that's one thing that every organization must ask," Greg says. "What is our vision? What is our unique product? What is our unique service? What is our unique contribution? Why do we exist?"

Answer those questions, set your strategies, goals and 30 day actions accordingly...and then follow through. "A lot of people who start businesses are visionary entrepreneurs," Greg added. "They have this great idea. They have a lot of energy... but sometimes, they don't work as hard as they need to in developing the specific how-to steps of the plan...Sometimes they can build too fast."

"There's a picture I saw years ago...a little goldfish bowl with a large-scale Asian goldfish inside. The bowl was cracked and water was beginning to pour out. The slogan underneath read, *Growth is only good if you're ready for it.*"

This is a lesson worth remembering.

Now, after goals are created and actions identified, we need to be sure we have alignment throughout our organization and accountability for performance, bringing us to the next step in our strategic planning process.

Aligning for Operational Excellence

You have a solid plan in place. You're ready to start talking about generating leads, hiring more help and marketing to your target audience. But before we do that, let's look at one last, yet critical, phase of the planning stage. Along with the 30-day action plan, this is the missing ingredient in virtually all strategic plans.

Let's talk about how you're going to deliver on your promises and ensure everyone is on the same page.

ALIGNMENT: THE OVERLOOKED INGREDIENT

Now, having convinced you of the importance of systems, I want to mention an equally-important but often overlooked ingredient that can make or break your move toward a systems-based business... *alignment*.

Yes... you've heard me mention it several times already, but let's dig deeper into what alignment really means.

Alignment is the consistency of message, content, tone and actions across each delivery mechanism, from executives and their staff to the ads, the packaging and the policies that govern the way they do business.

When a company has alignment, the employees are in "sync" and the various departments work together in unison, toward a shared set of goals. But without alignment, you'll hear comments like:

"We're not on the same page."

"We have no idea what he does in marketing."

"They're making my job harder than it needs to be."

Lack of alignment is what causes an employee to be surprised when he or she receives a poor performance review. And quite often, that's one of the first signs that alignment is absent... the employer is measuring the employee on standards and benchmarks that he or she either doesn't understand or isn't even aware of. So, when the employer hands out a poor performance review, the employee responds with things like, *"That's not fair"... "I do my job"... "It's not my fault"...*

And if management hasn't bothered to create alignment within the company, then the employee is right: it's not their fault. They have no way of knowing what's expected or what constitutes good performance.

As a CEO or business owner, it's your responsibility to embed this concept of alignment in your company, etching it into your corporate culture and requiring each and every employee to operate by its terms.

There must be a linkage of vision, mission, goals and actions from top to bottom. This increases the chance that everyone is on the same page, all of the time... and when they're not, it's much easier to pinpoint the problem. Of course, alignment isn't just about the presence of these elements—it's also about the intensity with which they are applied on a daily basis.

We utilize this Strategic Alignment planning and management system in our firm and in our coaching and consulting engagement with CEOs and business owners. Impressive improvements start to appear when everyone in an organization adopts the process. Everyone is on the same page and the entire team starts to reflect shared values and principles in the daily performance of their duties. We strengthen it further by ensuring that each team member has their own goal-driven agenda tied to the overall goals of the firm and that they understand their role within the company and how they contribute to the company's success.

And this alignment has a direct impact on our bottom line. Consider this excerpt from Thomas C. Powell's article in the Strategic Management Journal [1]:

1   Strategic Management Journal, Vol. 13, February, 1992

"When evaluating financial performance variance, strategic management researchers and industrial organization economists have emphasized industry factors, market share, generic strategy and strategic group membership. Organizational Contingency theorists have emphasized alignments involving environment and internal structure. This study integrates these perspectives, testing the financial performance consequences of organizational alignments, in context with the effects of industry, market share and strategy. In an empirical study in two manufacturing industries, it is shown that some organizational alignments do produce supernormal profits, independent of the profits produced by traditional industry and strategy variables. The results are consistent with the resource view of the firm: to the extent that alignments result from skill rather than luck, it is reasonable to regard alignment skill as a strategic resource capable of generating economic rents."

What this article is suggesting is that, by focusing on industry and competitive strategy variables, contemporary organization and strategy research has understated the role of alignment in producing sustainable competitive advantage.

In my experience, the sustainable competitive advantage of alignment is quite clear. When a CEO or business owner takes the time to constantly articulate firm values, operating principles and goals, it matters. When leaders get team members involved in the development of these values, principles and goals, it matters even more.

And when leaders sit down on a regular basis to help team members develop their own goals and show them how it fits into the bigger picture, you are not just building competitive advantage with less turnover… you're creating an entire culture within your company.

So, how do you create this all-important alignment?

It starts with clarity. In order for everyone to follow the same path, they have to be on the same page of the same planning guide.

One of the reasons that Vince Lombardi is such a legend is that he made sure that no one doubted or had questions about the mission of the team and their role as an individual contributor. As a result, the Green Bay Packers were a force to be reckoned with… and it's because they played the game as a team, each with their own specific job but also with an understanding of how that assignment related to the group's mission.

The second component is communication. In order to convey your mission and values in your staff, you have to communicate and that means sitting down with your employees on a regular basis to talk about challenges, objectives and how your company wants to move forward.

Of course, communication doesn't just stop with words. In fact, 90% of communication is said to be non-verbal, with 60% coming from body language and the other 30% being conveyed through tone. In terms of corporate communication, we're talking about action here. How your company interacts with its employees and its constituents as well as how your company, as an entity, lives up to the same standards and guidelines that you're imposing on your staff. Is yours an honest and honorable business for example, or do you cut corners and overcharge your customers whenever you can? Yesterday's article in the New York Times by a recently departed Goldman Sachs employee [2] makes my point: What's at stake is the soul of your firm.

Your employees may not say anything about it, but you can bet that such behavior affects the way they choose to perform their duties—even at Goldman Sachs.

This brings us to the last component of alignment: trust. In order for your staff to follow the vision you've conveyed, they have to trust that you're leading them in the right direction. They have to believe that you have their best interests at heart—not just the value of your stock or the amount of profit you're making. When they trust you, they'll follow you... and they'll do whatever it takes to help you create the most amazing version of the company you've envisioned.

The tools of alignment are Strategic Objectives, or goal setting, the 30 day action plan and your one-on-ones with those that directly report to you. Everyone within the organization does it the same way. Once everyone knows the vision, mission and critical success factors, they set their goals and actions, all consistent with core values. Then you manage for commitments and coach for accountability to insure progress is being made at the desired pace.

After all, it's one thing to create strategies and set goals. It's quite another to achieve results. You can make all the promises you want about

---

2   *Why I Am Leaving Goldman Sachs,* Greg Smith. http://www.nytimes.com/2012/03/14/opinion/why-i-am-leaving-goldman-sachs.html

the quality of your product, for example; but, if that product doesn't live up to expectations, your company won't succeed and there's no amount of marketing or lead generation that can change that reality.

Instead, you'll have to be able to do what you said you could do. You have to build your products, supply your distributors and service your market in a way that results in delighted clients, positive cash flow and long-term sustainability.

And to do this, you're going to need systems.

THIS IS HOW WE
DO THINGS HERE

S ome call them systems. Others refer to them as processes. The point is, you want to have a culture where everyone recognizes "This is the Way We Do Things Here," every time, without exception. This is especially true with respect to "what" you do. Deciding "how" you perform that task can either be part of your system or you can give team mates more flexibility.

Systems are what enable you to deliver your products on time. They are what allow your company to produce the same quality and service day in and day out. Systems make it possible for your team to be on the same page—working toward the same goals and using the same processes to get there.

And I can personally vouch for their effectiveness.

In 1989, I was sitting in my office when a financial advisor friend of mine came into the office, handed me a book and said, "You have to read this. You'll love it."

And he was right… It might well be one of the best gifts I have ever received.

The next day, I headed off to Miami for a week-long tax course, but I remembered to bring the book with me and I'm glad I did because doing so completely changed my idea of how to structure my business. I certainly spent a significant amount of time digesting that tax course, but I gained more about how to build a successful firm that week by absorbing Michael Gerber's *E-Myth* philosophy, realizing just how powerful having a few select systems could really be. To borrow a popular "today" phrase—for me it was Game Change.

His message spoke to me, touching my deepest beliefs and confirming the notion that performance is directly tied to process. Gerber's eloquent thesis is contained in these two points:

The Fatal Assumption: just because you understand the technical work required of a business, that does not mean you understand the business that performs the technical work; and,

The Franchise Prototype: in order to succeed, any business must be structured and organized around systems.

Since that time, Gerber has gone on to co-author numerous variations of *The E-Myth* for different industries. In fact, my good friends and coaching partners, Robert Armstrong and Sandy Fisch, co-authored *The E-Myth Attorney* with Gerber. Our common belief in the power of systems is one of the reasons my law firm has been a member of their organization, *The American Academy of Estate Planning Attorneys*, since its inception in 1993. Gerber's concepts and the Academy helped me create and implement systems for my law practice and I have lived by the power of these systems ever since. And, believe me, if effective systems can be created for a law firm, they can be created for any business.

So, having given you that testimonial, let's look at what happens when you *don't* have systems in place.

Randomness . . . discretion . . . variability . . . the enemies of quality control and profitability. And, don't even talk to me about loss of spontaneity and creativity. That's your head trash. You can be as creative as you need to be. Just be sure you focus it on having the most consistent, predictable and reliable fulfillment systems you can possibly create.

Without systems, each team member will create their own set of processes and often without much thought as to what is most effective or what in the best interest of the team as a whole. Tasks will be handled using whatever habits and beliefs the employee has picked up along the way and it's not uncommon to find employees duplicating mistakes they see others in the organization making because, "that's the way we've always done it." When I hear that it prompts a fairly serious discussion.

What this means is that you'll have a systems-based business whether you want it or not: the only question is, will the systems be designed strategically by you or will you wait to see what each employee comes up with on their own?

Choosing the former ensures that every detail of your company is attended to and every aspect functions the way you've envisioned it. Case in point: Today I am working from home. And, as I write this chapter, I receive an email from an attorney in our law firm. This is a new attorney and he wanted to let me know that he's decided how his phone calls should be handled.

Sorry… not in my firm.

That decision isn't within his purview. Instead, we have a system for how all phone calls are handled and his will follow that same exact procedure. If he wants to suggest a more effective system at our next creative planning session, we will welcome the discussion. Why is this a big deal? Imagine for a moment what our front desk would be like if we had different procedures for 20 different attorneys…

Yep… chaos.

Instead, we chose a single, uniformed system that ensures our clients always get the service they deserve and our attorneys always receive their messages. It works, it's efficient and the person answering the phone knows exactly how this aspect of her job should be handled.

Now, efficiency and effectiveness aren't the only benefits of having this kind of system in place. It's also a great training tool. Imagine that my receptionist is out sick and someone else has to fill in… having a set of documented procedures for handling phone calls ensures that the change in staff doesn't automatically mean a change in service.

Yes, I realize that this mindset requires a huge culture change for most organizations but it's one that needs to be made if you want your company to succeed, especially in these turbulent economic times when budgets are tight and competition is high.

If planning and philosophy are the foundation of your business, then systems are the materials you use to build the walls. And like the three little pigs, you can choose to use bricks or you can choose to use straw and I think we all know the consequences of choosing the latter.

You need systems that cover everything from answering your phone to filing documents to opening the mail to soliciting new clients.

Your systems should explain each system, step-by-step, on every task... what kind of accounting reports are run each month... how files are archived and sent to storage... how deals are negotiated and new marketing campaigns are launched... how emails are answered and how issues are handed off to other people or departments.

The more systems you have, the more predictable your company can be.... And when a company is predictable, you have more control over its performance.

In order to create these wonderful systems, you'll have to do some research. You may need to purchase new software, new hardware or even hire in some professional help to make sure it's all done right.

Having a systems-based business means that every department, every mission and every task has a set procedure for getting things done. And that procedure is the same every single time. You are saying, "This is how we do it here." You want detail. You want manuals with written processes and flow charts to illustrate how every task at that work station is handled when being done with excellence—manuals so complete that if a worker walked off the job, their replacement could sit down, review the manual and begin to function effectively and *immediately*.

To create these manuals and the systems that go in them, you'll need a keen understanding of your business, both as a whole and as each individual aspect that contributes to the bigger picture. You'll also need to be ready for resistance because remember, your employees already have their own version of a systems-based business and chances are, they won't like the idea of restructuring the way they do things, even when your way is better.

Now, are you wondering how you'll prevent these systems from becoming too rigid, perhaps irrelevant, in a turbulent environment? The answer is simple: you test them to verify they still lead to the highest possible productivity. And you do that by asking these questions:

- What are we doing we should no longer do?
- What are we not doing we should start doing?

Once a system is finely tuned and operationally efficient, the crossbar for changing it should be high, modified only if it leads to even greater efficiency and productivity.

KEEPING SCORE

Admit it... you're excited about setting up some new systems and creating performance alignment with your organization, aren't you? Of course, in order for those systems to work the way you want them to, you'll need to have a way to measure the effectiveness of utilizing this new approach.

After all, it's easy to *say* that something works great but, without the data to support that claim, there's no real way to know for sure.

And truth be told, nothing destroys an opinion like hard, cold data. Granted, numbers can be manufactured, and depending on how they were collected, they can also be disastrously misleading.

But in a performance management culture, you cannot manage what you do not measure. Measurement alerts you to potential problems before they become full-blown disasters. On the flip side, if you illuminate a performance standard by daily numbers, those responsible will focus more intently on its achievement.

And to accomplish this, monthly P&L statements are necessary but inadequate. Yes, you need the historical data. But you need more. To measure effectively, you need a prognostic approach so that you can plan for, and even predict, future outcomes. In fact, this is a point of distinction between our most successful CEOs and those who have not reached their goals.

To create this kind of measurement system, you first need to know and understand your revenue and expense drivers; in other words, a way to evaluate actions and behaviors that create each critical line item. In almost all of our consultations and coaching sessions with CEOs, we find that those in charge know they're making money, but they're not real clear on what exactly generates that profit. And because they don't understand what drives their revenue, or the appropriate marketing costs, or how to staff for current results and future expectations, they don't bother tracking these drivers; much less take the time to use them as a management tool.

Before our coaching calls we expect participants to send us an agenda of points they wish to address during our 30 minute call. One recent agenda item listed the last three years revenue and, on another line, his compensation during those time periods. Of course, you know. Rising revenue, flat compensation.

We spent the entire call helping the participant understand the importance of breaking down his numbers by applying best practice industry standards of different ratios to his business until he could quantify, then clearly articulate, why the outcome was occurring. At some point in the process, he will have to measure whether the utilization rates of current staff will allow him to reach his income goals.

Once you understand your revenue and expense drivers, you need to implement a system that incorporates your accounting and financial reporting with your company's goals and missions. If you want to increase your profit by 20% for example, your accounting department should be aware of this goal and your reporting systems should be set up to measure your progress.

A scorecard is a very useful tool that compares your daily performance to your benchmark objective. This scorecard system measures and tracks key indicators of your business... how many new clients you need or how much revenue must be generated, for example... how an unexpected expenditure affects your progress and what you can do now to prepare for potential setbacks in the future. Take your scorecard system one step further by incorporating your marketing metrics and client acquisitions costs and you begin to see the advantages your company would have with such a tool.

And finally, you need a system for collecting feedback, both from your clients as well as your employees. Honest feedback lets you know how you're doing. It tells you if you're meeting expectations and it also tells you if a process or procedure isn't working the way you'd hoped. You can then use this information to tweak the process, change the procedure or rethink the expectations you've created about your company.

CREATING AND PRESENTING YOUR BUSINESS PLAN

Now that you know where you want to go and how you will get there, there may be times when you have to present business plans to third parties—that is, lenders, partners, strategic alliance partners or affiliates. In that event, you will want to arm your Turbulence Thrival Plan with additional firepower. You will need to be clear about the purpose of the presentation, and have company credentials ready for examination. It's time to solidify your plan by committing it to paper. Despite popular belief, it's much more than just a collection of financial documents.

DEFINING YOUR PURPOSE

Business plans can be required for a number of reasons and for a variety of purposes. It's that purpose that will define how your plan is constructed.

In addition to helping you obtain funding from third-party lenders or attract investors, your business plan can also aid you in addressing other management concerns such as determining what resources you'll need to launch or expand your business or whether or not a particular new product or service fits with your overall vision and mission. Business plans can help you define agreements between your partners and create processes and procedures that ensure your business stays on track.

A good business plan can even help you create an exit strategy and set a value on the business for when you decide it's time to move on.

It makes sense then, that you would craft your business plan to suit your current needs, so you can start by asking yourself a few simple questions:

- What is your primary purpose for creating this element of your Turbulence Thrival Plan? Are you looking to secure outside financing from investors, apply for a loan, or establish your operational procedures to augment a written blueprint for your business?
- Who will see the plan? Is it exclusively for internal use or will others (i.e., investors and loan officers) also be reviewing it?
- Will this plan need to serve other purposes in the future?

Now, the reason that last question is important is that like the bigger Turbulence Thrival planning process, your business plan is designed to be an on-going project. Just as your company will grow and change over the years, so should the plan that defines it. If you know for example, that you have a desire to bring in a new partner down the road or entice private investors to help you expand into a new market, you can begin designing your plan to accommodate that new focus now.

BUSINESS PLAN ESSENTIALS

Once you've established your purpose, it's time to start gathering your data. Fortunately, regardless of what type of plan you're creating, there are a few components that should always be included and can serve as a solid starting point:

- **Executive Summary** – Your executive summary is basically the plan's introduction. It serves as the foundation for both the plan and the company that it represents. Your summary should include a rundown of what's presented in the plan as well as a company history, a description of your products and services and an overview of your facilities. Your executive summary should also include both your vision statement and your mission statement, and if you have specific plans for future projects or growth, those can be included here as well.

- **Management Team** – This section includes brief biographies of key personnel, including the founders, board of directors and upper management. You can also add information about how your company is structured and how the responsibilities are divided among key company leaders.

- **Services and Products** – This section covers just what it says – what is it that you're selling? What kind of products or services do you offer and what benefits do they offer your target market? Is your product copyrighted or patented? If so, include that information here. Do you have plans for new products and services in the future? List them out in this section, detailing any applicable timelines, obstacles or other variables that might affect seeing this product or service come to fruition.

- **Market Analysis** – This is where you'll talk about your target market—who they are, where they're located, how much money they make on average and most importantly, how you plan to get in front of this coveted audience. This section also includes information about your competition, the economy, your core marketing strategies and any obstacles you foresee hindering your climb to the top. You can circle back and include your SCOT analysis here as well. Include both strengths and weaknesses—what makes you better than the competition and likewise, what will prove to be a challenge that your company will have to overcome. Ideally, much of the data for this section will come from an entirely different plan—your marketing plan—and that's something we'll cover in Part IV.

- **Financials** – Yes, you still need to include some financial statements, even if you're not planning to secure a new loan or entice outside investors. And here's why: a basic financial analysis will help you allocate your resources and make realistic projections for future sustainability. Must-have financial documents include income statements, balance sheets and cash flow statements that both trend your historical data as well as project your future income. It may also be important to share a scorecard of key financial metrics. Keep your projections conservative and approach your financial picture from a worst-case scenario. This will ensure that you always have enough to meet your obligations and can survive despite those unexpected surprises we discussed earlier.

You're Armed With a Plan...Now What?

After spending so much time and energy in the planning stage, you might be expecting to discover a fully-functioning, successful business has emerged as your reward.

But you're not done just yet...

While you certainly might have the blueprint for building the next contender for the Fortune 500, you're not going to get there all by yourself. No, your plan is only as good as the people you hire to execute it, so we'll be focusing the next two chapters on how to build that kind of award-winning team. And pay close attention...

Because you're going to discover that staffing isn't just about filling empty positions and it's not just a certain skill set that will reveal the right person for the job. Instead, you'll need to learn to look deeper and hire your people for the employee that they can become (given the right circumstances and environment) rather than just the worker they appear to be.

In his book, *Good to Great*, Jim Collins sums it up nicely, by suggesting you put the "who" before the "what." Likening your company to a bus, it's your job as the bus driver to get the bus moving. But rather than simply tell your passengers where you're going, you'd do better to focus on your passengers first, direction second. Therefore his advice, you must have the right people on the bus.

"...*leaders of companies that go from good to great start not with "where" but with "whom." They start by getting the right people on the bus, the wrong people off the bus, and the right people in the right seats."*

This mindset suggests that there's more to creating a solid team than just hiring good people—you have to also ensure that you have the "right" good person in the right position and we're going to talk about how to do exactly that.

Obviously, by now you won't be surprised I want you to have a system for putting the right people on the bus.

So, without further ado... let's start finding and herding the cats.

SOME FINAL THOUGHTS ON PLANNING

Very early on, some of the companies didn't have plans. If you had a goal without a plan, you only had a wish. About five years after I got into the manufacturing business, we did the business plan. It was in the fifth year and it was very basic. I only had two key people at that time. The three of us went to Lake Geneva for about five days, then had our wives come up on the weekend. We worked out the plan together on a full-time work basis. It really hurt us that we were growing so fast, because we didn't keep up with the plan or update it. From 1993 through the end of 1995, we didn't have a plan that we were following and that got us into trouble.

We were never without a plan after that.

— **Dick Savage**
Retired, President, United Rotary Brush Corporation

Having a vision is important, but be willing to adjust that vision if need be. Start out the year with goals, but if things dramatically change, adjust those goals and go a different direction. We do a lot of hiring for local clients. As people stop hiring, we had to readjust. We had to keep our eye on the ball as far as our goals, but we developed a plan to assist our clients with employees they had to let go.

— **Linda Winlock**
Owner and President, Personnel Profiling Inc.

When you look at people who operate from emotions, they don't really get anything done. They're always kind of on the sidelines as far as making things happen. I think the reason is because most folks want to proceed in the absence of fear. Successful entrepreneurs cannot succumb to the presence of fear.

— **Kelly Brown**, DDS
Owner, Custom Dental

Systems are absolutely crucial to running any kind of successful business. Otherwise, it's chaos all the time. I first came to the understanding about the need for systems when I first created this marketing juggernaut on the estate planning side and had all of these clients coming in. We had people coming in the front door and we were trying to figure out how to get the work done. We recognized that without a clear system with everybody understanding what they were going to do and the exact way that we wanted to do it, the firm was going to be in chaos. That was my first realization… necessity is the mother of invention!

— **Robert Armstrong**
Co-founder of the American Academy of Estate Planning Attorneys

It gets people thinking—what can we do? How can we be the best we can be? And not only does that apply to clients, it also applies to people within the firm. If your people are pushing hard, let them have all the rope they can handle. Give clients the same thing, pushing hard, give them rope. I think that's another key with the success we have had—how can we give them something? How can we make this better? Not just make it look better, but make it function better, make it fit, make sure the operations and the functionality works well.

— **Bob Barnard**
President and Founder, Barnard Dunkelbert & Company

Minds are like parachutes... they function best when they're open. Culturally in our company, one of our core values is openness. We turned all of our core values into actionable statements but the issue of keeping an open mind means you sometimes have to absorb at a faster pace; you have to absorb a lot of things coming at you. Then, you have to take action. I've always said the greatest thing in a business is action—and that was when times weren't even this turbulent.

If you do nothing, you're no competition.

— **Bryan Beaver**
Owner and CEO, CarterEnergy Corporation

I am constantly amazed at how many CEOs can't read a financial statement properly. They rely on their accountant and if they're lucky, they ask a few questions a couple of times a year. It's so much more valuable when they can pick out the five things that are most important—the key indicators—the top five key indicators of whether we are doing the job right or not. There is a lot more to it than just revenue and profit. A lot of those measurements should be much, much more on the pipeline that ultimately leads to business opportunity.

That brings me back to the seven things that we learned after the exhaustive research we conducted—values, time, decision-making, strengths, relationships, habits and support structures. Those are the seven things that mater the most. You've got to isolate, think about, discuss, and debate what you are doing. How much time do I spend in each area? What is the time and percentage that I spend with relationships, decision-making, etc.? How many of these represent an internal focus and how many represent an external focus? Even a 10% change in your time over the course of a year will get you dramatic results... might even be the difference-maker in a day like today—in the turbulent market.

— **John Dudeck**
President, Guardian Equity Group

For the last 20 years, I have run my company business from what I call the **performance management system.** I meet individually with the key people that report directly to me on a weekly basis, so things are monitored on a weekly basis. That answers the question regarding frequency. Obviously, end of the month statements aren't done weekly, but there are things that are done that can be monitored weekly. Also, key performance indicators can be reported to me on a weekly basis. We look at every position in the company and we work with them to develop their own objectives. Those are being monitored as frequently as they can be monitored. The last part is T which is time-bound. If something can be monitored weekly, it is monitored weekly. For example: every week I get a series of reports…for example, new members who join us and the number of members that are attached to each independent business adviser. Those are things that can be monitored weekly. Again it depends on the frequency of when things can actually be monitored but everything is built on that system.

— **Bill Glazer**
President, Bill Glazer Consulting

Unless you have really disciplined and rigorous processes in place for investment decisions, operational, or for anything you want to achieve in the company, you are setting yourself up for failure. If there are processes and rules in place, then you have to have people in place who with respect those rules. Then, the top people can feel comfortable in delegating and letting folks do their job. They know those processes and rules help those folks know when they are supposed to come to the senior guy, senior committee, or the executive—whatever you have in place—and let them know that they have an issue. When the people in your organization understand, "get it," and are experienced enough to know when they are supposed to counsel; that gives confidence to the top workers so they can be doing other things and not worrying about the execution of every project. We spent a lot of time thinking through, tweaking, and putting these kinds of policies and procedures in place.

— **Mike Glosserman**
Managing Partner and Chair of the
Executive Committee of The JGB Companies

PART III
PEOPLE
Finding and Herding the Cats

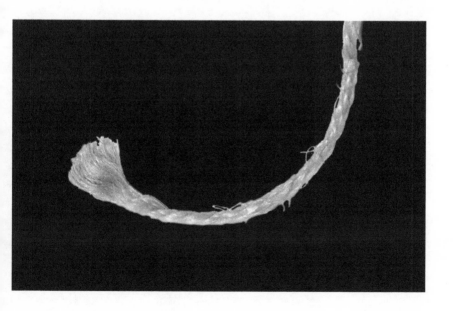

"If you pick the right people and give them the opportunity to spread their wings—and put compensation as a carrier behind it—you almost don't have to manage them."

— Jack Welch

Hire for Attitude and Strengths — Train for Skill

Just as we develop processes for other parts of our business, we need to have a hiring process as well. Sadly, most of our coaching clients have no rational system for hiring excellent team members. It seems to start and end with placing an ad. Be clear—the ad is very important. But it's only one step in a very meticulous, thorough process. In today's hyper-competitive, turbulent world, hiring is too important to the success of your company to be left to chance. Hiring mistakes are very disruptive and expensive.

Somewhere along the way I learned the lesson that good people are free. By that I mean that the right person with the right attitude and strengths will more than pay for themselves, once trained for skills. You can train someone to use your phone system for example, but having a friendly and energetic disposition is something you just can't teach.

Unfortunately, many executives have the notion that they can, in fact, change the nature of their employees and because of this belief, they've essentially auctioned off the positions within their company to the lowest qualified bid. Imagine their surprise then, when that employee doesn't prove to be a valued member of their team. That's because it's much more important to have the best possible people on your staff than it is to quibble over whether you're going to pay $45 thousand a year to a mediocre candidate or $50 thousand to the employee of your dreams.

Staffing your company with smart, ambitious people who have complementary strengths and a great attitude is always the better choice.

But what about experience and skill sets? Don't those things matter too? Absolutely. But the right attitude will go a long way in distinguishing your company from the rest of the pack. When this type of employee suffers a setback, they don't blame others. They don't complain and they don't try to hide the mistake. Instead, people with the right attitude take responsibility for their actions... they make corrections and they find ways to be even better than they were before.

Of course, in today's economy it's all too easy to staff your company with people who are content just to have a J-O-B. But in most cases, these are not the people that are going to be with you for the long-haul. They're in it for the paycheck and when their circumstances change—or a bigger paycheck comes along—they'll be gone.

And, you'll be back at Square One.

As American Academy of Estate Planning Attorneys' founder Robert Armstrong says, "Being in business isn't a short-term proposition."

Yet so many CEOs treat it that way.

In one of our discussions, Steve Harmon, partner at Centriq Training, recalls an employee who took his program to a competitor and marketed it as his own. "Our program was branded with him. The public knew his name more than they knew our company.... We should have terminated this guy on our terms long ago, but we didn't. This was just a pure greed factor on our part. We weren't happy with his performance, character or values, but we were happy with the profit he brought to us. We turned a blind eye to his shortcomings and chose profitability. That really burned us."

And, maybe that's the key. It takes courage to make the right hire and even greater courage to choose values over profit when evaluating whether you should keep them.

We're all going to make a few mistakes along the way. We're going to hire someone who interviewed great or came highly recommended, but then never quite fit in with the rest of your team.

And, when you make those mistakes, prune that person faster than you would a dead limb on a beautiful tree. Most of us have heard it before—hire slow, fire fast.

You're growing an organization as strong as a Redwood and you don't need someone spreading their version of Dutch elm disease on your team. Instead, isolate and eliminate. And do it fast. You have entirely too much to do to spend valuable time trying to provide the cure to mediocrity…in any form.

Focus on Company Strengths

As CEO, it pays to focus on your individual strengths in order to maximize your personal effectiveness. We've just seen how it pays to take strengths into account when staffing your team. It also pays to have your organization focused on its specific strengths to maximize wealth creation or shareholder value. A few days ago, I noticed an article in the *Wall Street Journal* that illustrates this point. The article described the decision of Hartford Financial Services Group, Inc. to abandon their annuity business and put their life insurance up for sale. The article made it clear these steps were taken so the company could focus on its Property and Casualty insurance business.

Apparently the action was taken due to pressure from large shareholders who have been disappointed with Hartford's recent stock price performance. One was quoted as saying that Hartford's main problem remains a "lack of interest from P&C Analyst and P&C Investors in Hartford's best in class P&C business due to its affiliation with unrelated, low return and complex businesses" such as annuities. And the article went on to point out that this was just the first step. My question is, why did it take pressure from shareholders to make this happen? Did the CEO lose touch with how shareholders feel about focus? So, the point is that we should focus on individual and organizational strengths—on those activities where we can come close to being first in class.

Staffing and organizing your company for strengths always starts with the question "what can this person, or this company, do?" rather than "what can we, or he, not do?" The idea is to feed opportunities and starve problems. And remember, the standard of any organization is set by the performance of the leader.

Now, having convinced you of the importance of organizing your company and hiring good people based on strengths they can contribute, let's talk about how to accomplish that goal consistently and effectively.

KNOW WHAT YOU WANT

Earlier, we talked about having the right person in the right seat on the right bus... and here's where that comes into play.

You're not just looking for a new receptionist or someone to process claims... what you really want is a collection of attitudes, abilities and skills that allow this person to fill a specific position AND perform with excellence. You're looking for critical thinking, patience, persistence, friendliness, salesmanship, creativity, leadership and/or anything else that might help your employee excel in their job. Most of all you're looking for someone who has a strong need to excel and will do so within the scope of your core values.

So, before you go looking for a new team member, you want to be sure you know who to look for. Someone who is naturally passive and doesn't like conflict might not be the best fit if the position calls for them to troubleshoot and resolve customer complaints, no matter how experienced they are in company procedures or how pleasant their telephone etiquette might be. Likewise, someone who's naturally assertive and gets bored easily may not be your best bet if the position will have them sitting behind a desk all day processing orders, even though they might know your shopping cart system better than anyone else in the department. Experience and skills definitely matter, but choosing the right employee requires you to go much deeper.

Putting the right person in the right seat on the right bus means that you've matched that person's abilities and personality traits to the requirements of the job. It means that you first identify the capabilities and skills that make an employee fit within your corporate culture and then you start looking for traits that will help the employee excel in a specific job.

For example, if your corporate culture is structured and conservative, hiring someone known to be flamboyant and contemporary probably won't fit well. It doesn't matter if they're well qualified for the job—the drastic difference in personalities is going to make it difficult for them to fit in. So, the first thing you'd look for would be someone who likes the quiet and structured environment you've created and then you'd start looking for traits that are specific to the job in question.

Are they good at problem-solving? Do they interact well with others? Go find the person best suited for that position. Start by building a position description with requirements and attributes described as if they are being performed with excellence. Now from time to time, a person referred to us is a perfect fit and after going through our hiring process, we feel confident we don't need to look further. Without this kind of referral, you'll have to recruit, either through an agency or on your own. How you start is crucial.

IT ALL STARTS WITH AN AD

Since your first encounter with a candidate is quite often your ad, it makes sense to use this opportunity to attract some serious contenders.

And you do this by creating expectations.

When I write ads for our jobs, the copy is designed to speak to just one person. During follow up one on one interviews I always ask, "What was it about the ad that inspired you to respond?" I'm often told they felt the ad was speaking to them; that it laid out opportunities and professional challenges they were specifically looking for. Creating expectations of excellence and high performance continues from your first contact with the prospective team member, throughout the interview process, into the job offer, and certainly as part of your team.

Most companies view the recruiting and hiring process as a necessary evil—something that they "have to do." As a result, little effort is put into this task, other than sorting through resumes and conducting multiple (and usually identical) interviews in a one-on-one setting. But this is a wonderful opportunity to strengthen your team and grow your business. Think about it: hiring a new employee is no different than the college coach looking to recruit a new star player. Yes, the coach goes after the talent. She looks for excellence. And, if the coach is smart, she selects the players that best fit her system. She is crystal clear about the role she is looking to fill.

And, just because she finds that star player doesn't mean the recruiting stops. This isn't a one-time exercise—the coach and her team are constantly scouting for the best possible talent for their program. During March Madness for example, you can rest assured no coach is making personnel decisions based on whether a player is a freshman or senior. That should be your mindset as well.

Typically, a position description outlines the tasks performed in that position. But here's a better approach:

Instead of simply listing the tasks to be performed, organize them around the candidate's areas of responsibility. Make it come alive by writing a description that tells the candidate not only what needs to be done, but also what will be happening when it's performed with excellence. This allows the position description to become a tool that creates expectations and sets the benchmarks for an excellent performance.

At my law firm for example, our Director of First Impressions does not have a task that reads, "Answer the phone." Instead it reads, "I answer the phone within the first three rings 90% of the time with a pleasant, helpful greeting: 'Parman & Easterday, good morning, this is Vikki... how may I help you?'"

And, as you might imagine, given the expectation, this standard is consistently met.

Writing your position descriptions in this manner ensures that there is no confusion about expectations and performance standards. Then, when that new candidate accepts your offer to join your company, have them sign that Position Description. Now you have a position contract with performance standards.

LEVERAGE YOUR TIME

Finding and hiring the right people is time-consuming. We started this practice in the mid-1980s. From Day One. I was committed to finding only the most qualified team members to join my journey. The problem was simple: time. I didn't want to delegate the important task of hiring (and neither should you); yet, I was having difficulty finding time for one-on-one visits with 15-20 candidates. So instead, we implemented a group interview process and used specific steps, or filters, to eliminate the applicants who, for whatever reason, didn't meet our expectations. I believe I "borrowed" the idea from reading *Nuts*, a great story about Southwest Airlines written by its former CEO Herb Kelleher.

Here are a few of the ingredients of our system. To start with, candidates are required to take specific steps at specific times in order to qualify for the group interview. For example, "To attend this interview, call 800-725-8000 between the hours of 7 P.M. and 9 P.M. to let us know you are coming.

Leave your name, phone number and what it was about the ad that sparked your interest in this position."

You cannot imagine how many fail. That was just fine because following simple instructions is a fundamental job qualification. Over the years, candidates have blatantly disregarded instructions by calling our main office number during the day and tying up our team with twenty questions. We're courteous, of course… but obviously, those applicants are out. Each requirement along the way acts as a filter to eliminate a poor fit.

We also ask them to submit a handwritten response to our ad, telling us why they believe this position is the right one for them. This allows us a little insight into what parts of the job description appealed to them the most and also gives us an idea of what their expectations are so far. Why not a typed response? Because you can't spell-check a handwritten note and you can't have someone else write it for you.

If they follow directions and show up for the group interview, they have now passed a number of elimination filters and they've also demonstrated confidence. Surprisingly, many would-be employees aren't comfortable in this kind of setting and again, that's fine. We're looking for someone willing to abandon their comfort zone, who doesn't mind a little "in your face, one-on-one" competition and won't hesitate to speak up and be seen. This filter eliminates candidates that didn't meet our criteria.

This filtering process continues until we finally arrive at two-three individual interviews. By then, I have a much better idea of who I'm talking to. From this point, we can get down to the serious business of whether this is a person for us and whether we are a firm for them.

The irony of a group interview is that those who participate enjoy the process, but that's not something that "just happens." You have to make it happen. One year we had over 100 people apply for a marketing director position. We divided them into four groups of 25 and we encouraged them to use the event as a networking opportunity by bringing their business cards and sharing them with the other attendees.

After all, we were looking for that one special candidate, which meant that many good candidates would be unsuccessful. It turned out to be a great event and at least two people secured other positions from contacts made during our interview process.

We always include staff interviews as part of our process, allowing finalists to meet and interact with our team members in the office. Getting feedback from your staff about potential new hires accomplishes four things: 1) it fosters the team-spirit we keep talking about; 2) gives your staff a sense of ownership and responsibility in making a high-quality choice; 3) it ensures that you don't miss anything; and 4) it gives you a chance to see how the new person and your existing employees will interact together. By the way, if any staff member strongly objects to a candidate we give great weight to their opinion and probably won't hire them.

DO YOUR RESEARCH

Assuming that your candidate has passed all your filters and tests, you might think that it's time to make an offer... but not just yet.

Before you invite someone new into your team, you need to check their references. And you need to do it in writing.

Checking references is one of those things that many business owners overlook. It's time-consuming for one and truth be told, most business owners don't expect to get anything useful out of a reference check.

After all, how often is it that someone gives out a bad reference?

But that's exactly why you need to do the research. And to ensure you get the answers you're looking for, you should create a written reference "questionnaire" that the responding party can simply fill out and mail back.

And here's what you want to know:

Start off with the basics: verify employment dates, the candidate's position and duties and of course, the reason for leaving. But then get a little more specific. For example, you also want to know if the candidate is qualified to assume certain responsibilities. The only way to know this is to ask. Give the previous employer a list of duties or skills that your position requires and then ask if they believe this candidate could handle such a position.

Is the candidate a team-player? Do they work well on their own? Can they self-manage? Depending on your position, the inability to work without constant supervision might be a serious problem. And on that note, ask the previous employer what type of management styles the candidate encountered in that job. Did the candidate seem to work better with certain styles over others?

Ask about attendance and dependability. Is the candidate someone who likes to take initiative or does this person perform better when the steps of a project are laid out for them? What are their strongest qualities and how did they respond to constructive criticism?

Obviously, not everyone will be willing to fill out such a questionnaire, but it never hurts to try and any response you get could offer some insight that you didn't have before. If a response isn't received, feel free to follow up with a phone call—sometimes employers are willing to say things over the phone that they wouldn't put in writing.

Most importantly, pay attention to what isn't being said. You should usually be able to tell when someone is trying to dance around giving a straight answer. If that's the case, then there's no need to push—the "non-answer" answer tells you what you need to know.

PROFILE YOUR PERSONNEL

No matter how much time we spend interviewing someone, we have to remember that we're still only seeing a small piece of their personality. After all, your applicants are well aware of the importance of this interview, so you can bet they're on their best behavior.

But before you extend an offer, you want to be sure that the person you're hiring is truly a good fit… and to do that, you're going to have to dig a little deeper.

One of the best ways to accomplish this goal is to use a personality test. Some even assess a candidate's capability. These tests can assess not only the applicant's personality type but also how they'll fit within your corporate culture… and as we've already seen, that's a crucial component to your success.

But there's a secret to using personality tests effectively. Different tests measure different components of a personality, so you'll want to start off by being sure you're using the right test.

The profile we always use and recommend is offered by Linda Winlock's company, Personnel Profiling. Her assessment and services for selection and development are superb. You can find out more about Linda at the end of this book. Others have found the DISC, Kolbe and Strength Finder programs very useful as well.

The other thing to remember when employing these tests is that you can't just use them on new applicants. In order to truly understand how a new hire would work with your existing team, all of your team members would need to take the test as well in order to have a complete picture of the personalities within your team and how they work together.

PUT YOUR OFFER IN WRITING

Once you've made your decision and picked the perfect applicant, you'll want to put your offer in writing. Yes, you should first make the offer in person and hammer out any salary negotiations or other conditions and terms. But when everything is finalized, a written confirmation should always be sent.

Why?

Committing your offer to paper now avoids confusion down the road. It ensures that both you and your new employee have the same understanding of the position and all that it entails. Your offer letter should include not just the salary you'll be paying but also the employee's title, the benefits and the position description detailing the tasks and expectations that come with this position. Things change fast in turbulent times, so be sure to include flexibility to handle newly created responsibilities in the position description. If this is a lengthy list, then, you may want to condense the initial offer into a shorter letter and provide the new employee with a longer supplement document to cover all the extras.

Your offer letter should also include any requirements that must be met before employment can begin and any contingencies that affect employment continuing.

Of course, such a document could easily be construed as an employment contract, so if that's not your intent, you need to take steps to ensure it can't be used as such. An at-will statement for example, in accordance with your state's employment laws, is a must and you'll also want to omit any words or phrases that suggest long-term employment. Chances are your attorney or legal department has some boilerplate language they'll want you to use and having them review your final draft is always a good move.

You should also ask them to sign and return the letter as an indication of their acceptance… and then give them a specific date by which they have to respond.

THE 100-DAY PLAN

It's been written that nothing is more important to a CEO's success than how he performed during the first 100 days. It's been said the same is true for new U.S. presidents. During that time, their political capital account is at its peak. It's equally true for all new team members.

Have a series of specific actions for a new team member to accomplish during their first 100 days. Some will be administrative—signing W-2 forms, getting set up for the company retirement plan and other benefits and learning how to use the copier and various technologies. Others will relate to training and understanding company processes. Make sure you cover it all. Cultural indoctrination is critical. In our firm, we require new employees to read three books and report on them at staff meetings.

You also need a feedback system to be sure they are spending their time on the right things every day. Having them send you or their supervisor an email at the beginning of the day outlining what they want to accomplish that day, followed by an end of the day report on what was actually accomplished, the time spent on each task and what they need from you (or their supervisor) is a great feedback tool. We have found it very effective at helping get new team members indoctrinated to our culture. It helps them develop results-based habits.

Of course, finding the right people and getting them started off on the right foot is just half of the equation—now you need to figure out how to manage them successfully… and like everything else, you start by having a good plan.

But before you can manage others, you have to learn how to manage yourself… and this is where execution resides.

LEADING THE CATS –
MANAGING YOURSELF

With this chapter, we're going to start exploring a different aspect of leadership—the aspect of management. And here's where things get a little dicey. Because before we talk about managing others, we're going to address how to manage you.

And that's an entirely different animal, indeed.

As the CEO or business owner, you're responsible for choosing the destination, charting the course and setting the sails. But in a management capacity, it's your job to see that the destination is actually reached and that requires a very unique skill called execution. Fortunately, with your Turbulence Thrival and Strategic Action Plan in place, you are off to a good start.

EFFECTIVE EXECUTION

Execution is what separates one executive from another, one company from its competitors, one nation from the rest of the world. Execution at its most basic level is about getting things done… on time, on budget, as agreed—a concept that can be quite a challenge for many companies and the executives who lead them.

And that's because they're missing some of the elements that are vital to effective execution.

In their excellent book, *Execution: The Discipline of Getting Things Done*, Larry Bossidy and Ram Charan offer several elements that are crucial to meeting your goals. Discipline, for example, allows you to complete your task in spite of the variety of distractions that threaten to take your focus off your objective.

Discipline leads writers to write every day, often at a specific time. When they do so, they ensure that nothing else is allowed to interfere with that time. Those in great physical shape are the way they are because they work out every day and eat properly at every meal. Athletes who achieve greatness do so because they work on improving their skills faithfully… no exceptions. These are examples of discipline and it's a trait very few people truly possess. And, take note—even the greatest of them has a coach or trainer. Do you?

But discipline is a trait you need if you want to see the company you've envisioned become a reality in the here and now.

Another trait that's often overlooked, or, in many cases, downright ignored is the element of speed. Watch someone with effective execution skills and you'll notice that they attack new tasks and projects with a vengeance because they know that letting them wait will cause an array of problems down the road.

- In our law firm, for example, we have a process for handling a new client. Here are the assumptions:
- I retain one client per day.
- For each client, I complete a Client Information Form (CIF) that reflects precise details of that client, their family and their wishes for an estate plan design.
- The CIF is delivered to a specific person, who then processes the retainer and updates the client's records in our database.
- The CIF is delivered to the appropriate paralegal for plan preparation, within one week after the client is retained.
- The document production assistant needs the CIF and the special drafting provisions no later than two weeks prior to the final signing.

- We deliver the completed plan to the client, ready to be signed, 30 days from the date they retain us.
- We do this work for a fixed fee.

Now, when everyone performs their part of this matrix with effective execution, things run smoothly and profits are made. But, if an attorney sits on his work for too many days, it's not long before a bottleneck begins to accumulate and production suffers. After a couple of weeks, the information becomes stale and the attorney will forget certain details about the case. In an effort to catch up, he makes mistakes.

What's worse, when all this old work finally does make it into our system, there is a ripple effect. Now everyone has to deviate from their workflow system in order to handle this sudden influx of new work, because remember... we've got an agreement with the client to deliver a completed estate plan within 30 days. This is how a crisis is born out of a lack of discipline.

So, even though this attorney might be retaining 75% of his prospect meetings, his performance is disruptive and as a result, it's costing the law firm dearly. Not only does it reduce profitability, but it also jeopardizes morale and puts client service excellence at risk.

Now, put this same attorney in a management capacity. How do you imagine his lack of execution affects the rest of the team?

Once again, we see the ripple effect and it's not long before this kind of mediocre commitment to execution is infecting the entire team. Want to take a guess how long it takes us to stop meeting that 30-day client commitment?

So, having established the importance of effective execution, let's talk about how to achieve it in your organization.

FITNESS, VITALITY, ENERGY

Making a commitment to excellence requires much more than just a promise. It also requires some of that discipline we mentioned earlier, but in more than just the professional side of your life.

In order to meet those deadlines and reach those objectives, you need to be alert and prepared... something you cannot do if you don't take care of your own health. Yet, commanding a company frequently requires you to work long hours and endure a great amount of stress—two things that are sure to sap you of energy and decrease your overall productivity.

Knowing that, you can take steps to ensure that you're always up to the challenge.

Making a commitment to integrate a regular exercise routine for example, ensures that you not only stay fit but also that you have a healthy way to relieve stress. Likewise, eating a balanced and nutritious diet ensures that you'll always have the energy you need, even for that spur-of-the-moment 5 o'clock meeting.

But we're just getting started. After all, your physical health is just one aspect of your overall well-being. There's also your emotional wellness, your relationship wellness and, of course, your financial health, each of which has a distinct and lasting effect on your ability to lead and execute effectively on a daily basis.

It's not unusual for example, to see stressed-out executives going home to stressed-out households. And the reason is simple: the executive hasn't yet found a way to leave his work at the office and as a result, his entire family suffers. This constant barrage of stress will eventually lead to burn-out, and that's when the executive will stop being effective at all.

Having balance in your life is vital. And there is a positive correlation between your emotional and physical well-being and your business success. The professional follows the personal. It is crucial to avoiding this performance trap and enduring some of the difficulties that come with being on top. In his book, *The Healthy CEO,* Dr. Larry Ohlhauser talks about the importance of discovering success outside their career in order to enjoy success within.

"You are a leader in business—a success," he says. "But are you successfully leading your life?"

TIME MANAGEMENT

As a busy executive, your time is everything. Every minute of every day is precious and filled with possibilities. Why is it, then, that so many executives waste more time than they actually use productively?

In our constant state of "GO!," we frequently jump from one crisis to another, working late and multi-tasking at a whole new level in order to meet all those deadlines we've deemed critical.

But working at this pace continuously ensures that we won't be as productive as we'd like to be and we won't have time for the more interesting aspects and challenges that come with being in charge.

The key then is to figure out how to manage your time effectively and true to form, I've included some ways to do just that:

Know Where You Spend Your Time

The key to this exercise is to agree not to lie about the data. Keeping a time log allows you to ruthlessly identify where you spend your time and what your potential time wasters might be. Have someone else observe for a day and record the outcome. If you're honest about the exercise, you'll find many opportunities for increased time leverage. This is the starting point to a more effective and profitable use of your time. Without facts to confirm hunches, anything you do is pure guesswork.

Prioritize

Ours is a world filled with distractions. But we have to find a way to balance those distractions with the other things on our plate if we want to feel a sense of accomplishment at the end of the day. One way you can do this is to learn the difference between what's important and what requires your attention right now.

President Eisenhower put it this way: "What is important is seldom urgent and what is urgent is seldom important." Using this philosophy, Eisenhower created a two-pronged matrix (often called the Eisenhower Matrix) that allows executives to evaluate a task based on its true urgency. And on a side note, this same matrix was reintroduced in Steven Covey's bestselling book, *The 7 Habits of Highly Effective People*.

Important (low urgency, high importance)	**Critical** (high urgency, high importance)
Distractions (low urgency, low importance)	**Interruptions** (high urgency, low importance)

Using this matrix, tasks can be classified according to a scale of importance. Tasks that are essential to achieving a goal for example, may rank high on the importance scale but not so high on the urgency line. Likewise, an emergency may rank high on the urgency line but lower on the scale of importance.

Using this grid, you can then start allocating your time according to the projects and tasks that need it the most. And, what about everything else?

To answer that question, let's look at the third secret to good time-management.

Delegation

We talked briefly before about the risks of micro-managing and failing to delegate. Now, we're going to bring that topic full circle.

In order to manage your distractions and fully utilize your strengths, you must be able to hand off many tasks, yet know they will be handled. That means that you need to be able to delegate work to your staff. To do that with confidence, you're going to have to give them some room to grow.

Delegating is a crucial component to an executive's success because it allows you to focus on the tasks that capitalize on your strengths and truly require your attention while knowing that the rest is being handled effectively and efficiently.

So, how do you decide which tasks to delegate?

The answer to that question will depend both upon the task in question and the abilities of your staff. A paralegal, for example, is capable of much more than just typing contracts and filing petitions at the courthouse. But if her supervising attorney does not provide adequate training or give her the opportunity to master more complex tasks such as drafting those petitions and negotiating those contracts, then the attorney won't be able to confidently hand those tasks off when time is critical and the attorney has more than he can handle.

The solution then, is to start looking at how you spend your time, retain those tasks that match your strengths or you feel you must keep, then consider which tasks could be handed off—to those with proper training and matching strengths. Doing it now gives you the luxury of training your staff properly rather than inducting them with a crash-course lesson down the road.

What is Your Time Worth?

One of the best ways to decide which tasks should be delegated is to figure out how much your time is really worth. After all, if a task could effectively be done by an employee with a lower hourly rate than yours, then it makes sense to delegate that task and free up your time for more demanding projects.

The first step is to calculate the dollar value of each hour of your work day. Now, there are a variety of resources on this topic, all providing you with similar formulas to calculate the value of your time but let's use a very simple method for purposes of this chapter: take your annual compensation and divide it by the number of hours you'd like to spend working.

Notice I didn't say to use how many hours you're working now—instead, factor in time off for all those vacations you haven't taken and assume that you don't bring work home with you every weekend. Find a reasonable number of hours—a number that allows you to spend time with family and friends and one that allows you to focus on your personal life as much as your professional persona—and use that as your calculation. This is how much one hour of your time *should be* worth.

The next question you have to ask yourself is how much of your time are you spending on tasks that could be done for far less? To say it another way, all of your hours must be spent on activities that generate revenue in excess of your hourly worth. Are you starting to view the items on your to-do list somewhat differently?

Focusing on the Task At Hand

The best way to ensure that you perform with excellence is to give a task your full attention at all times. Unfortunately, this is impossible to do if you multitask, a habit that can actually decrease your productivity and guarantee mistakes. Many studies confirm multi-tasking is impossible. You can only do one thing at a time. If you're texting while driving, you are either texting or driving. Focus to completion is a far better method of achieving desired results. And, it satisfies the importance of speedy completion. Interruptions slow down everything.

Multitasking makes concentrating difficult because your mind is trying to juggle multiple tasks at the same time. As a result, you're thinking about the staff meeting while you're writing the sales presentation while you're negotiating with a client on the phone and none will reflect your best work.

Instead, make a list of the things you want to accomplish and then—one by one—work them off your list—to completion—expeditiously.

The "Scheduled Task" List

In Part I we talked about setting goals. For proper alignment of vision, mission and goals, a majority of actions you take each day should relate to your goals. And since we're talking about lists, having a daily to-do list that ties back to your 30-day action plan is essential to effectively managing your time.

Here's a great tip for improving time management. Calendar your tasks. What's that? First, prioritize your tasks. Then, schedule the most important tasks on your calendar and treat them just as you would any other important appointment. This is a powerful time management strategy.

That's because despite your best efforts, a few distractions are going to interrupt you throughout the day. Some may even be critical, requiring you to stop what you're doing altogether and change gears completely.

Without a scheduled task list of things you want to accomplish, you'll lose your train of thought. You'll move from one distraction to the next because there's no plan in place for you to follow. Remember how important it was to set goals for your company? Well, the same applies here. A scheduled task list is your roadmap to small success stories. Use it wisely and you'll find you're more productive than ever.

Create an Advisory Board

There may be nothing you can do to increase your likelihood of success more than being accountable to someone, or a group, for your daily actions. Some of us don't like hearing this because it makes us feel vulnerable. After all, we created these businesses so we could be our own boss, right? Forget that. Unless you are very unusual, nearly unique, you will benefit from having to account to someone. Two great ways to do that are to create an advisory board for your company or hire an executive coach…or both.

Many small privately owned companies are benefiting from the resources that an Advisory Board can offer. The benefits can be substantial, while the costs are low, creating a great return on investment. The following is an overview of an advisory board and how it can help owners of privately owned companies.

What is an Advisory Board?

An Advisory Board is not a Board of Directors, which has a legal fiduciary responsibility to owners and shareholders. A Board of Directors also has ultimate control over the CEO of the company. They can hire and fire the CEO, determine compensation, etc. On the other hand, an Advisory Board is typically a group of professionals, often chosen for their expertise or influence in the industry or for their overall business judgment, sometimes in areas where they bring strengths and skills not possessed by the owner. They are utilized by the company in order to offer advice and guidance to the CEO and senior management. The Advisory Board members do not have the legal responsibility or liabilities associated with a Board of Directors.

There are many benefits that a properly formulated Advisory Board can offer:

1. Provide a sounding board for the CEO as the strategic direction of the company is determined, and adjusted over time. The Advisory Board does not create strategy for the company, but will provide advice and guidance to the CEO as the strategic direction is formulated.

2. An outsider's perspective is provided to company management. This can be especially important if the CEO of the company has limited experience outside their industry.

3. Members of the Advisory Board offer specific skills and experiences that the CEO does not have within the company. This could be in the areas of finance, marketing, technology, etc. They typically have much more experience in their field of expertise than anyone within the company. The company could not afford to hire this level of expertise on a full time basis.

4. Typical Advisory Board members have inside connections within their industry that can be of benefit to company management.

5. Advisory Board members do not have hidden agendas. They are not protecting their position within the company. They provide objective guidance.

Even the small family-owned business can often benefit a great deal from the independent perspective provided by an Advisory Board. If there are tensions between different family members that are preventing the company from moving ahead on new initiatives for example, the Advisory Board can serve an invaluable role in breaking these logjams.

The Advisory Board should be structured to meet the specific needs of the company, and the desires of senior management. To determine this, ask these questions:

1. What areas of expertise do the CEO and senior management team lack?
2. Are there specific industry contacts or relationships that need to be developed?
3. How might these needs change in the future?

When evaluating specific candidates, the chemistry between Advisory Board members and Senior Management is critical. A collegial environment should be sought in order to benefit from everyone's expertise. Advisory Board members must all feel comfortable in an advisory role. They should recognize that they are not running the company, but have a strong commitment to supporting the CEO. This could be difficult for some Advisory Board candidates, who would prefer a "command and control" environment. These issues must be discussed during the interview process.

Expectations must be set, and must be clearly understood by Advisory Board members. The time commitment required from Advisory Board members can and should vary over time, but some general guidelines should be set. How often will Advisory Board meetings be held (monthly, quarterly)? An additional time commitment from Board Members between meetings should be expected. If it is expected that a Board Member will help open doors for the company, then this should be clearly discussed.

Once a strong Advisory Board is established, company management will have the benefit of a committed group of professionals who can help make a good company great. In our rapidly changing, hyper-competitive global economy, an Advisory Board will enable any company to substantially improve their performance.

Work With an Executive Coach

Today more and more business owners and executives are realizing the merits of utilizing the services of an executive coach. The primary responsibility of the executive coach is to challenge you, help you identify blind spots, focus on strengths, evaluate the team, ask questions, help design strategic plans and encourage the executive/owner to create an environment that leads to desired goals. Their greatest contribution comes if they have a system that holds you accountable for outcomes you say you want to achieve.

This role is growing as it becomes more and more apparent that being the owner of a private company is a lonely endeavor. Having a trusted advisor, someone who has no agenda other than helping you set and achieve goals, business and personal, is a tremendous asset.

So, now that you're feeling confident about keeping yourself on track, let's spice things up a bit and add staff members to that equation.

LEADING THE CATS —
MANAGING OTHERS

I f your goal is to build a business, you'll need a team to help. We've already talked at length about hiring that team; now let's talk about how to manage them for excellence.

The first thing to understand is that you'll need a slightly different skill-set than you would in a leadership role. Leaders for example, strategize and motivate others to move in a specific direction. As a manager, however, it's your job to oversee the day-to-day tasks that will propel your company forward. In short, leaders inspire; managers implement.

Now, any good manager can tell you that these two roles aren't mutually exclusive... to be a good manager, you certainly need to be able to "lead" your team and, likewise, a leader isn't a leader if they don't understand the aspects of good management.

But all that said, at the end of the day it's the manager's job to see that things get done and to do that, you need to understand how your team works.

Creating this clarity and having each person understand their role and how they best contribute is not always an easy task. People confuse their roles and without clarity, it is virtually impossible to create accountability.

This is especially true during turbulent times when your world can be turned upside down on a moment's notice and team members need to fill multiple roles.

ORGANIZATIONAL CHARTS

Now traditionally, organizational (org) charts have been utilized for this purpose, giving management a way to get a "top-down" view of their company and begin the process of clarifying roles and responsibilities. All of us have seen the chart—a series of vertical and horizontal hierarchical boxes, each filled with someone's name and the title they hold.

This becomes especially important when you consider the impact that outsourcing has on today's corporate structure. I recall a conversation I had with Norm Stewart, the legendary long-time basketball coach at the University of Missouri. He said his goal was to have everyone on the team understand their role by the time they entered conference play each season. This is also true in business, regardless of whether your employees are on-site or working online in a virtual setting.

In theory, the org chart is supposed to function as a management communication tool but in reality, most org charts are never used and are seriously out of date. And there's a reason for this—other than showing who reports to whom, most managers don't see any value in them.

But used correctly, org charts can actually be a powerful management tool and also serve as a reminder of how important each staff member is to your overall objectives. Correctly implemented, an org chart can also be a very effective decision-making tool. The concept itself is sound—you just need a better chart.

First and foremost, your chart needs to be updated, because if you haven't touched the chart since your business began, there's a good chance that the people and positions represented are no longer accurate.

Then take your org chart one step further... after all, there's no rule that says you can't create a chart that also depicts the different teams within your company. And what if you included blocks to show workflow and authority? Think about it: it's nice to know who's "in charge" of the department, but wouldn't it be better if you also knew who was actually responsible for a given task or project?

Some charts don't even list staff members past a certain level of management, probably because there's a large number of employees and to do so would require constant updating. But think about what message that sends to your staff... is it really any surprise that our workforce doesn't feel kinship with the companies they work for?

Granted, you don't want a chart that's so complex it's impossible to read, but you do want a chart that clearly demonstrates how your staff contributes to the success of your company... and then you want to display that chart prominently where everyone can see it.

We recommend you organize your org chart by functions first, not by a person's name. This will do wonders for performance. It may seem like a small thing, but when someone sees their name associated with an important function, they start taking ownership of performing said function. It's also a perfect example of Deming's System of Profound Knowledge.

His system says that before you can transform an organization, you have to first transform the individuals within it, and this transformation comes from understanding the system that drives the organization and their responsibilities within it.

A properly erected org chart is the first step in this process. I also include it as part of my Turbulent Thrival Plan and attach it right behind my 30-Day Action Plan. Understanding how the departments and staff work together and how an idea is transformed into a tangible product or service is the difference between being part of a team and just working for a company.

THE MANY FACES OF MANAGEMENT

Just as people exhibit a variety of different personalities, managers exhibit a variety of different leadership styles. Traditionally, there were four basic styles of management, each with their own distinguishable character traits:

- **Autocratic** – Leadership from the top, down, having little concern for the ideas and opinions of subordinates.
- **Paternalistic** – Leadership from the top, down, but with the intention of doing what's best for the employees.
- **Democratic** – Leadership by committee; everyone has equal say in how decisions are made.

- **Laissez-Faire** – Hands-off style of management, allowing subordinates to make the majority of decisions.

But if you dig a little further, you'll find that other management styles have been identified and labeled as well—here's just a few that I've picked up along the way:

- **Servant** – Leadership through support and encouragement of subordinates.
- **MBWA** – Management by Walking Around… literally.
- **Visionary** – Leadership by inspiration, defining only the "what" and leaving the "how" to subordinates.
- **Coaching** – Leadership through development and encouragement of employee growth.
- **Affiliative** – Leadership through teamwork.

Now, in case you're wondering which style is the *right style*, the answer is none of the above… and all of the above. As the CEO or business owner, there will be times when you need to take at least a semi-autocratic stand and make a decision. Granted, you'll want to temper that decision with a paternalistic viewpoint, but ultimately you are the captain of this ship and it's up to you to chart its course.

There will also be times when you'll want to take a hands-off approach and many, many times when you'll want to present a more democratic style of management. And of course, leadership through teamwork, inspiration, encouragement and personal growth are always good options as well.

And that's really the secret of effectively managing others: figuring out how to mesh these styles together to fit the culture of the organization as well as both the personalities of your team and your own personal beliefs and values.

A tip: Be consistent and communicate an expectation of excellence at all times.

BUILDING YOUR TEAM

I actually overheard this first in our office between two ladies a few years ago. I had no idea what they were talking about. I asked. Here's what they told me. When a romantic relationship moves to a new level, there is frequently a "conversation." The conversation that says "we might not yet be engaged, but we're exclusive now and that means there are certain expectations we're both expected to abide by." I immediately applied the concept to the management process.

The same is true when someone new joins your team—you need to have the conversation with them and set expectations from the get-go.

The rules that govern the relationship between supervisor and employee can, and should be, relatively simple... but there are a few things that I recommend you always include and they go something along these lines:

First, I agree to give honest and sincere feedback as quickly as possible. I'll try to do it in a positive and constructive way. If, because of time constraints or other demands in my life, I don't give you this feedback as majestically as you'd like, my apologies in advance. But no matter what, I won't lie to you and I will give it to you as clearly and straightforward as I know how.

I'll also listen to your feedback as well and when we work together, the golden rule will govern our interactions.

Seems simple, doesn't it? Ironically, these basic agreements are the difference that will bring you closer to excellence than 98% of your competitors, because most don't even bother having the conversation... much less give thought to which rules they want to invoke.

Knowing the Generations

And on the subject of hiring the right people, you should also be aware of how the generations fit together within your corporate culture. Tony Lewis is an outstanding Vistage (formerly TEC) Chair in the Kansas City area. I was a participant in his Group 112 for a number of years. In my recent discussions with him, Tony shared a few important points about understanding the different generations in the workplace and how their values can impact your organization.

As to mistakes in hiring he observed that many business owners tend to hire people for what they know—their technical expertise—because we want them to do something special in our business. Then, we often end up getting rid of them for their attitude or who they are.

His next observation was that because of all the evolving different environments that are out there in a business—whether it be accounting, technology, administration, engineering—it is critical to hire people who are learners. Then, when evaluating strengths and where someone might best fit into your organization you have to consider their generation. He talked about a recent speaker at one of their Vistage meetings who had documented the DNA of the five or six generations that are in the workforce. Every 20 years you get a different generation. He detailed the documentation all the way back to the fourteenth century. You can see the cycle. It cycles every hundred years by twenty years at a time.

The GI generation, the baby boomers, generation X-ers, Y-ers, and, now the millenials—if you mismatch them to a job, no matter what their profiles indicate—you'll have problems. A GI's mindset says, "tell me how to do it and I'll do it every time. I'll be loyal. I'll be here for 40 years." But someone from the millennial generation isn't going to get that mindset and if you put the two together, you'll find that they struggle to accomplish goals because they're too distracted by the generation gap that governs the way they work. In the end, both will likely become frustrated and unproductive... and they'll believe it's the fault of their team member.

The Communication Feedback Loop

I confess that I learned this concept through trial and error, but since learning it, I've never used anything else. Do the same, do it consistently, and you'll quickly become a more effective manager.

It works like this: First you discuss the issue. You then reach an agreement about the next step or the desired outcome. You and the other party verbally repeat your understanding of the agreement. You resolve any conflicts that might arise and restate the agreement again. You then ask the other party to confirm the agreement via email and you respond to that email with "correct" and include a blind copy to yourself.

Finally, you convert the email to a PDF and save it in the employee's file.

This process provides you with a nearly flawless way of documenting agreements and objectives with your team members. It achieves a degree of clarity that's often missing in most organizations. Plus, it's fast, dependable and creates a paper trail that can be used for accountability.

Now, here's where this concept becomes extraordinarily powerful: I insist that all my direct reports use this system with their direct reports and I am cc'd on the emails. Hard copies are kept in folders on a public drive on our file server, so if one of my direct reports leaves or changes responsibilities, there's never a question about what objectives or performance standards they had put in place for their team members.

This feedback loop also lets team members know that you're paying attention, that even what may be minor agreements are important to you and the company. The Heisenberg Effect reminds us that what gets observed gets changed and often improved. This loop is another example that confirms that principle.

GOAL SETTING AS A MANAGEMENT TOOL

Not long ago, I asked a couple of team members to create performance standards for their respective positions. They had a difficult time doing it, but working on that project gave them a new appreciation of what they did, what great performance looked like and how it should be evaluated.

And this same process should be followed with each and every team member.

Before you can set goals, you first need to understand how to measure them. The team member responsible for meeting the goals should play an active role in this determination.

Asking your team members to define the standards of excellence for their respective positions forces them to look at that position from an outsider's point of view. What skills and duties does this particular job require? How should their performance be measured when it's time for a review?

And what level of performance would be required to achieve the excellence your company strives for?

Having your team members contribute to this process ensures that there are no surprises at review time. If they contribute to setting the standards, then they're well aware of how they're being measured and what it will take to receive a favorable review.

Likewise, you'll have a better understanding of what it is each team member actually does and, more importantly, what it takes to get that job completed to satisfaction.

Once these performance standards have been agreed upon, it's time to set goals and, again, the team member should be a key player in this process.

Now, you'll likely find that you have some employees who resist the goal-setting process. They know what they need to do and they know how to do it... why spend time writing it all down and discussing it? If they resist, it may indicate a reluctance to be held accountable.

But whether you (or they) realize it or not, they're probably setting goals already... they just haven't thought about it in those terms. But I guarantee that if you have someone on your staff that is the kind of employee you *want* on your staff, they're tracking their performance in one way or another.

Goals help us stay focused, they help us measure performance and they help us grow as individuals. The key to goal-setting with your employees (and with yourself) is to set goals that are achievable but also challenging.

You want your team members to grow and learn just as you do. You want them to become better, faster and smarter because as they improve, so does their performance within your company.

Your goal in this respect is to be their coach—coach them to a position where their gifts will naturally be revealed. Encourage them to reach a little farther, try a little harder and believe a little stronger.

The result is that you end up with smart, savvy employees who feel a kinship to you and your company because you took the time to work with them, encourage them, and demonstrate your belief in them. It was there they discovered their true potential. Do this, and then ask, "What kind of company do you suppose you'd have with a staff like that?"

THE DREADED QUARTERLY REVIEW

Let's get this out of the way...no one likes quarterly reviews...period. Managers dread holding them as much as team members loathe receiving them. That's why they happen so seldom. And, if they happen they are typically organized and handled poorly. Here's why.

People do not like feeling judged. Plus, they have been trained to link reviews with discussions about compensation. If the review is all about what they did wrong and there is no "raise," or compensation is not discussed, why should it surprise us that the team member has just experienced a de-motivating session with her supervisor? That has to be fixed and it starts from the beginning of employment.

The notion that review sessions are linked to compensation has to be ended. This should be made clear to all new hires. Since you didn't take the time to do it then, or did not know to do it, do it now. Sit down with direct reports and make it clear that reviews are about performance and performance only. Then have your direct reports do it with their direct reports and repeat until this is clarified throughout your organization.

While you are at it, make sure that everyone understands that their current compensation is based on a pact that they perform their current duties with excellence. Mediocrity is not acceptable. Make it clear that adjustments to compensation will depend on their commitment to continuous improvement of their contribution to the bottom line. And that those decisions will be made apart from the quarterly review.

Now that we understand why quarterly reviews seldom work and what to avoid, let's take this communication concept one step further.

One-on-ones with your direct reports are the most important management task you can perform and the lynch-pin to the success of your Strategic Alignment Plan and therefore your company. And between you and me, quarterly is not frequent enough.

I recommend you hold them once a week. Thirty minutes should do it. If not that often, then hold them bi-weekly or monthly, at a minimum. Schedule them on appropriate calendars and treat them with the reverence you would a meeting with your best customer. Never miss or reschedule a one-on-one. Face to face is best but if either of you is out of the office that person can call in.

The one-on-one is about your direct report, not about you. It is to gain a sense of progress on goals and improving performance.

As a guideline, the review should cover these points.

1. The Look back — the team member's overall reaction to the past quarter? This leads into a discussion of what went well and what fell short.
2. The Assessment — what specific progress was made on goals?
3. The Shortfall — what fell short? Why? What corrective actions were taken? What concerns do you have?
4. The Look Forward — the recommitment to complete prior goals and the creation of new goals, all with appropriate timelines.
5. Skill Building — what one skill will you improve this quarter that will increase your contribution to the firm's goals?

Over time the one-on-ones provide the opportunity for you to make it clear that achievement and additional compensation is to be measured against objective criteria of contribution and performance. This is best accomplished if jobs are defined and structured impersonally; otherwise the accent will be on "who is right?" rather than "what is right?"

THE DAILY MEETING

When he was mayor of New York City, Rudy Giuliani utilized a daily 8 AM meeting with his department heads to get control of his day and create a method to process challenges in a timely manner. The daily 8 AM meeting became the core of his management method. It served many purposes, including decision-making, communication and helping him stay on top of the multitude of issues facing the CEO of any organization.

Maybe even more important, as Giuliani stated in his book, *Leadership*, "...it kept me accountable."

A daily meeting of key team members is certainly worthy of your consideration. Most organizations utilize a weekly staff meeting and that may be enough, if handled correctly. The more important question is what should that meeting accomplish?

These meetings have two primary goals: First, identify issues that need to be resolved, make decisions and assign responsibility. This provides each participant a forum to share any news or issues they're facing within their area of responsibility. This is especially important for those instances where one person needs something from another, and the failure of that happening affects the ability to complete the task.

The second goal is to make time available for the CEO/business owner to address any important issues that affect the organization as a whole. It's also the perfect opportunity to talk about vision and expectations. Ideally, these meetings should be positive and upbeat, so save the criticisms for a personal one-on-one whenever possible.

Each meeting should also have a written agenda. Someone is assigned the responsibility for taking notes, clarifying actions, transcribing the notes and distributing them to each participant. Any unresolved matters are automatically added to the next week's agenda, and, absent an emergency, in front of any new agenda item.

In our law firm, we hold a weekly staff meeting and conduct it according to the guidelines above. In addition, a number of team members send daily email reports. When they arrive in the morning, they send me their to-do list. At the end of each day, they let me know what was completed, how long it took and list their goals for the next day. And the process begins again. As I mentioned earlier in the book, this is especially important for new team members during their first 100 days.

There are a number of benefits of this approach for both the CEO and the team member. It serves to create focus and helps manage priorities. It gives team members an opportunity to raise issues that occur between weekly meetings or areas where they require assistance. The report also provides the CEO a feedback system of what is and isn't working in each area of responsibility.

It identifies whether agreed-upon processes are working and, as an added bonus, it allows the CEO to quickly identify team members that are overloaded as well as those who could assume more responsibility.

Complacency

This is the arch enemy of excellence. In my observation of CEOs and business owners through the years, our one-on-one coaching engagements and our Peak Performer groups, complacency stands tall as a reason businesses falter or fail. And, to be clear, it's the CEO's fault.

People, let me say it straight—effectively leading and managing a team is hard work. You've fought hard to own a successful business, to become CEO of a company. It would be easy to take a deep breath and relax a little as you recognize what you've accomplished. Fair point. Do it—deep breath, say "Well done." Now get back to work. You cannot ascend to the pinnacle and let your guard down for a single second. Eternal vigilance over processes and people is mandatory. There are no short cuts.

It often starts out by excusing a less-than-excellent performance and justifying it by the fact that someone has been a valuable member of the team for 15 years, or the misfeasance "is not that big a deal," or it's a one-off exception, or she'll make up the time down the road, and the list goes on.

Pretty soon the plan you had in place is the plan they have in place and you are the CEO in name only. What's really happening is that you're losing your courage to hold people accountable, to inspire them to be their best regardless of circumstances.

This is one reason why performance standards need to be in writing. If you go to the gym and do not write down the times, the sets, the reps and the weight I'm betting that at some point there is less intensity, therefore less effectiveness, in your workout and therefore your fitness. Professional sports teams, even professional golfers and tennis pros, are relentless in setting performance standards then filming and measuring actual performance against the desired objective. A professional slips one bit, you know what happens.

Ask Peyton Manning, the only four-time winner of the NFL's MVP award. A combination of (supposed) age and injury made him vulnerable and I hate to say…expendable. Yes, the stakes in the NFL are extraordinarily high. But this is your team. If you are willing to allow complacency to manage your company, you should trade managers.

LETTING THEM GO

Of course, there will be times—no matter how well you manage and coach—that you'll have to deal with team members who just aren't working out. In fact, Dan Kennedy says at some point "…they all go lame." And in the litigious society we live in today, letting someone go is not always an easy thing to do.

But that doesn't mean it can't be done. First, some legal advice: Find out what options you have concerning termination under your state law. Even if you are in an "at will" state, check anyway.

If you're faced with the prospect of having to let someone go, you'll want to first make sure you've done everything you can as their boss to help them succeed. This goes back to communicating your expectations and coaching them with regular feedback and performance reviews.

Resolve any training issues and make sure your staff has all the tools and resources they need to do the job the way it should be done.

And then document when they don't.

But don't just secretly keep a file of bad behavior. Instead, bring the employee in and ask them directly to change whatever behaviors need to be changed. Let them know that you'll be documenting their performance and that it must improve in order for their employment to continue.

Outline what constitutes improvement and be specific... their production must increase by X number of batches per week or their attendance must improve by X, Y and Z. Be honest and open about their performance and encourage them to participate in this conversation. Are they having difficulties completing the tasks in question? Is there something they need or something you can do to help them achieve the excellence you're looking for?

Once the parameters of performance improvement have been established, use the Communication Feedback Loop to confirm. This ensures that there's no misunderstanding and that you have a proven paper trail to support your decision to fire down the road... assuming that it comes to that.

As part of your agreement, set interval times to meet, review and discuss. What areas (if any) show improvement? What areas do not? Are there any new circumstances or challenges that affect the employee's ability to do the job? Are there any new concerns or issues noted in the employee's performance that weren't discussed before?

Restate the agreed upon standards for improvement and, once again, follow the Communication Feedback Loop to ensure that all parties are on the same page.

Failure to make progress may require a probation period. That, too, must be clearly communicated and documented.

This process accomplishes two things simultaneously: first, if you do decide to fire the employee, you have a lengthy probationary period that is full of continuous feedback and coaching and is documented and corroborated by everyone involved.

It's the second benefit, however, that makes this process so worthwhile. Quite frequently, the employee isn't initially aware of the boss' displeasure in performance (yes, even when *they know* they've been slacking) and as a result, the reprimand or firing comes as a complete surprise. But that's not the kind of ship you're running, is it? Making the employee part of the documentation and review process makes it easier for him or her to recognize where they're falling short and take corrective action. The result is that you can often avoid firing anyone and instead end up with a better employee for your efforts.

And that's a win-win any way you slice it.

THE GOLDEN RULE

While all these concepts will certainly help you become a more effective and efficient manager, the truth is managing others is never easy and even the best managers will make some mistakes along the way. Mea Culpa.

How you handle those mistakes is what will determine how well your team can move past them and go forward.

Remember, in a management capacity, your role is multi-faceted. You're still responsible for leading the team but it's also your job to coach them to excellence. And that means treating them with the same respect and consideration that you would want given to you.

One thing you must not do is throw your people under the bus with a customer. In one of our coaching firms it was reported one of the attorneys was overheard telling a client, "I don't know why that work hasn't been done. Karen was supposed to have completed it a week ago." As it turns out, Karen had no idea what the attorney was talking about. Aside from her justifiable anger, her respect for the attorney took a nose dive. That is a fatal flaw.

My Dale Carnegie mentor Dick Roberts used to say, "If you lay an egg, stand back and admire it." If you mess up, (wo)man up and take responsibility. If there's something you want, say that too. The more honest and open you are, the more cohesive your team will be and the farther your company will be able to go.

Never underestimate the time required for the effective management of a team or the difficulty of the task.

Finally, regardless of circumstances, treat people with dignity, even if the other party does not return the favor. Don't get me wrong. You don't have to run from a fist fight if circumstances require it. I'm just saying you should take the high road when it's available. It's often not well traveled.

Some Final Thoughts
on Managing Others

Be very selective. Look at hiring people and investing in them the same way you would look at the best things in a company. One of the first criteria that I use is after I have been in their presence for 20 minutes is to ask myself, what has happened? Have they challenged, affirmed or given me an opportunity to really share and teach them? Or, are they all about and full of themselves?

Vividly, I recall one revealing interview. There was this one guy... and I asked him to tell me about the biggest failures or setbacks of his life. He said, "I haven't had any." At that moment, the conversation was over. I was courteous and all, but I went back to his boss and said, "I can't coach this guy, I can't do this." It is important to find out the failures in a person so you can discuss, work on and bring them along... so you can move forward. They have to be honest with themselves.

— **Ed Allen**
Retired, Rear Admiral, U.S. Navy

One of the first things I've come to realize is that hiring people is not one of my strengths. Over the decades, I've been in business running

133

my own business... I have hired and fired so many people. The people that I thought coming in were going to be great hires oftentimes are just the worst. People I thought would never make it turn out to be the most incredibly loyal and productive employees. So, I come to the task with a great deal of humility.

One of the things that we always do is, for the first 90 days, have a person send daily emails letting us know what they plan to accomplish that day. Then at the end of the day, we have them write down what they actually accomplished and whether there's anything they need from us in terms of resources or mentoring that would help them along. That's been extraordinarily helpful because it starts people off on the right foot, knowing that they're accountable.

We have incredibly loyal employees and staff and they have been with us for a long time. We have very, very little turnover in our company. So, you have to treat people right, you've got to take the high road in everything that you do—whether it's with your vendors, with your clients, with your employees and staff... whoever it is. Always take the high road. Recognize that being in business is not a short term proposition.

— **Robert Armstrong**
Co-founder of the American Academy of Estate Planning Attorneys

Finding and keeping good people should always be the number one priority of an organization. I believe strongly that past performance predicts the future, though it's not hard to determine someone's capabilities.

I don't believe that you can really change someone, but I do believe that you can influence their behavior through a very careful and ongoing communication of what is expected. That's probably evolved. At one point, I might have thought when you get your people and you let them do their job, the importance of communicating expectations is the evolution key. But, I have always known that it all starts with character. That becomes more and more important as you go forward. If you don't have character, there is no quality that can be worth the risk. To keep the people, you are ultimately going to be looking for the loyalty and dependability and integrity.

— **Mick Aslin**
Chairman, Alterra Ban

I'm probably a little bit of an old-school guy. When I start building a team, I think you have to have people that you can have double trust in. In exchange for that, you've got to be prepared for them to trust you. You've got to be able to make it through the valley with that team as well as through the good times. A lot of people in my industry hire people and fire them at the drop of a hat—thinking that they can be replaced. We can see that all over town and all over this country... where people will hire some real high-powered gunslingers. They'll make a bunch of money for the company and for themselves, but then when times get bad they're let go. That's not my philosophy at all.

I think you've got to build your team.

— **Carl Edwards**
Partner, Price Edwards & Company

The thing that I have discovered is that I don't need to be making all the decisions. I don't need to control everything. I don't need to be involved in every decision. I figured out a long time ago that if I am the smartest person in the room, we're probably in trouble. So, a really good leader is somebody that can gather people around that are a lot smarter than he or she.

The other thing I've learned is I don't think people expect you to be the smartest person in the room. They expect that when you are confronted with facts, you will make a decision and accept responsibility for that decision. I think a lot of leaders make the mistake of feeling that they cannot show any vulnerability to their associates. They feel they always have to be right. They think they have to be the ones that are technically more proficient than their associates. I've discovered that's just not true. I don't need to make every decision and I certainly don't need to be the smartest person. As a matter of fact, the very best thing I can do, and the most honor that I can pay my associates is to admit that I don't understand, to ask for help to figure things out. I don't think people are at all nervous by those kinds of vulnerabilities in a leader.

I think that's how organizations go down rabbit holes. People figure out pretty quickly what the boss wants to hear. Then, if the boss is unwilling to ask a good question, is unwilling to show vulnerability, if he has to be right, and has to have the final word... people figure that out pretty quickly.

Then, the only response you'll get is what people feel safe telling you—that is, what they think you want to hear and that leads the organization down an erroneous path.

— **Stanley Hupfeld**
Chairman, INTEGRIS Family of Foundations at INTEGRIS Health

If I was a new CEO or owned a business, the first thing I would do is meet with everyone one-on-one. I would say to them, "Folks, go about your business, unless, of course, there's some radical surgery that needs to be done. Keep going about your business. I don't know enough yet, but, I'm going to listen very carefully. I hope that you'll be forthright when I ask questions. I didn't learn much from success. I learned far more from failure.

My job here is to make sure that we win so I am going to count on your experiences. To win we have got to have the right team members and the right strategy. I'm probably going to come to you and ask a few open-ended questions every once in a while. I won't guarantee I'm going to do what you say but I'm going to listen." My favorite questions are — and I don't care what level they are in the organization—what do you love about working here and in your job? What do you like least about working here and in your job? And if you were me, what would you do different around here?

— **Tony Lewis**
Chairman, Vistage Advisory Groups

It doesn't matter what business you're in, your employees represent your business, not only at work but away from work. If people know that you work at Parman & Easterday, if it's known they work at Parman Chevrolet or the local bank, in the mind of the public they are that institution, they represent that business. How well they do it will be remembered long after a specific transaction.

When you're out in the community, your every action reflects on your company. That's the reason it's so very important to find the best employees you can. You always need to know more about your business than anyone else. That's why you own it or are CEO of the business. But, when looking for employees you still aspire to hire someone that's smarter than you are and who will have a sense of stewardship about how they represent your company.

— **Avis Parman**
Retired, Vice President and Board Member of the Business and Professional Women's Foundation

The break-downs start when the entrepreneurial type sales people start changing our systems, believing they can customize things better. They don't like this or that piece. They are going to put a new piece in. Every time I allow that, the whole system breaks down. They start bastardizing what I know needs to be in that packet. Standardized sales material is very important in terms of the systems.

I am open to anyone who can improve whatever they are doing, but they have to prove to me that it is an improvement and not just a distraction, something that serves as an excuse for, or distraction from, what they are there to do. Every change has to be justified by better numbers. If the numbers prove it and it's a change that will benefit everyone, you can bet I'm going to change, absolutely.

Every job description, policy and procedure should be documented in a procedure manual. We have a person on staff that does this with excellence. He is organized. He supports cross-training. He follows people around and has people document every single action from turning the key in the morning to turning off the lights at night. He literally walked through and systematized all the way down to the entry level— how to make the coffee, how do a back up. So, if someone should walk out or we had to let someone go, we have the system in place to train the next person. Systems are very critical in businesses where there is an entrepreneurial type leader. So many times, this type of leader is the deal maker and does not pay attention to the people or details that are a very important part of building a business. You must have a back-up plan in case something catastrophic happens with the person in charge of that department.

— **Dennis Curtin**
President, RE/MAX Mid-States and Dixie Region

Just yesterday I was thinking of the lessons we've learned living in turbulent times. We are both pilots, and the main thing they teach you to do when flying—lesson number one—in any kind of an emergency: fly the airplane. In a business, or when leading a city as I did as Oklahoma City's mayor—you have to lead. Do your job and lead. When Katrina happened, the fatal error that President Bush made was that he should have been there on the ground. He should have been visible—leading. He led in a wonderful way on 9/11. On 9/11 they told him to go and get in a bunker. He refused. He said, "Our people need to see me in the White House leading." Then, he went to ground zero and led in a wonderful way.

People expect their leader to lead. They don't expect their leader to do everything. The leader needs to be visible. The leader needs to instill confidence that he is there, he is on the job, and he is "flying the airplane." He is running the business. When the tornado hit Oklahoma City in 1999, Glenn Deck was the city manager and fire chief at the time. He told me that we had a command center in south Oklahoma City with lots of people everywhere. He asked, "You know why I feel good about this deal?" I asked, "Why?" He pointed at me and said he felt good because we were there.

And we were there, on the job and visible. I went out and walked through neighborhoods that had been devastated. I took rubber gloves and water and gave them to people who had just lost everything because that's what they needed. They were amazed that the mayor would just be walking through the neighborhood climbing through the debris to help them. That's what people want. They want to see their leader functioning; not panicking, and not hiding.

In a business, bad things happen. You are going to lose major clients; your industry is going to change. If the leader sits there, and says, "Just cut expenses until you make money," well, you can't cut expenses all the time. This doesn't always work anymore.

The world has changed. You have to adapt your business practices to the reality of whatever the market is at this given time. Get the facts and make a decision. A friend of mine (a mentor) told me years ago, "Get the facts, get all the facts, and then, face the facts. Make a decision and then follow through—now."

I may make a wrong decision. But then I get to make another decision.

— **Kirk Humphreys**
Chairman, The Humphreys Company

PART IV
PROMOTION
Growing Your Business
By Building Relationships

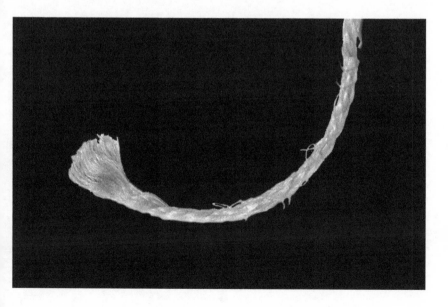

"If you wait until there is another case study in your industry, it will be too late."

— Seth Godin

THE IMPORTANCE
OF MARKETING

When I was in the banking industry, we used to joke that "marketing" meant installing one more phone line or changing out our logo and letterhead. Lawyers operated under much the same mindset, as did many other businesses who were accustomed to clients just "walking through the door" on a regular basis. And when you're in a business where people come to you, the whole idea of marketing and selling just seems irrelevant.

Add to that the fact that competition was confined to your immediate geographic location, and it's easy to see why many business owners never gave marketing a second thought.

Of course, those days are long gone.

The internet opened up the marketplace, forcing today's business owner to re-evaluate how they connect with their customers. Statistics show that over 90% of the population considers the search engines to be their first and best resource for finding new products and services. So, the moment your prospect sets out to find a solution to a particular problem or need, they are instantly inundated with a massive amount of information by simply "googling" their subject.

At this writing, for example, a search for "broom" returned over 44 million results. "Interior decorator" netted 1.6 million and "waffle iron" gave me 1.8 million. And in case you're wondering, the search term "attorney" returned a whopping 86.8 million listings.

Obviously, your prospects aren't going to weed through all those listings to find the best one. Instead, they're going to rely on the search engines and their assertion that the search results are ranked according to usefulness and relevance, meaning that the top listings—those on the first page—are also typically the best choices.

And for this reason, those 90% relying on the search engines don't typically click past page one… meaning that your business has to be on the first page of Google if you want to be seen.

This also means that your competition is no longer limited to the guy down the street—instead, you have to worry about companies located across the country, around the globe and even virtually on the World Wide Web. One of my clients owns an online bank—no brick and no mortar at all. And if that isn't bad enough, price isn't the only consideration anymore. Yes, there is still overwhelming pressure to commoditize everything, but consumers are smarter and savvier than they used to be. They'll often choose value over a cheaper price if the proposition is strong enough.

In short, the marketplace has changed. And your business will have to change with it if you want to succeed.

Ironically, marketing is often the first thing to go when times are tough. It's as if business owners see a strained bottom line and instead of thinking "generate more income," they immediately look for ways to simply cut costs. But if you're not marketing, you're not reaching your prospects—those people who have the power to literally save your company from hard times by boosting your bottom line with more sales.

The problem is, not many business owners truly understand the concept of marketing… at least not in a way that allows them to capture and promote the value of what they have to offer.

When we ask our coaching and consulting clients to explain what business they're in, the answer often revolves around producing their particular product or service. A manufacturing company makes a brush for the machine that sweeps airport runways and streets. A banker loans money and offers solutions to grow your savings by paying competitive rates of interest on deposits. Dentists repair teeth, doctors treat illness and lawyers set up practices to help people write a will, get a divorce or negotiate a contract.

In almost every case, the business owner believes they are in the business of making their product or service. But this thinking is much too narrow and too conventional for today's hyper-competitive marketplace.

The truth is you're not in the business of making your "thing," whatever that might be. Instead, you're in the business of marketing and selling the thing you make. See the difference?

My law firm isn't just a place where legal services are provided. It's a marketing company that just happens to offer business, estate and elder law planning services to its clients. This is a dramatic shift in mindset and one that will help you begin to see the *value* of the services your company provides. Understanding that value then allows you to develop marketing strategies that position your company ahead of the competition, putting you on the road to success. Same for our coaching and business owner consulting firm, Notch It Up Strategies. It isn't a company that helps executives and business owners be more effective leaders and managers. It, too, is a marketing company that generates clients who want to improve bottom line results through the improvement of specific skill sets.

And there's that word again… *value*. But what exactly does it mean?

Years ago, I was introduced to Robert Collier's books. His *Letter Book* talks about the importance of understanding the 'conversation' going on in the mind of your prospect. This conversation is how they weigh the pros and cons and decide on their next course of action. The specifics will differ of course, depending upon the issue in question and the circumstances of the individual, but regardless of all these variables, those conversations always lead back to one core concept: *why should I buy from you?*

Answer this question effectively through your marketing and you'll make the sale. Miss the mark and, well… you get the idea.

Of course, in order to answer that question, you have to answer some questions of your own… questions that define the audience you're targeting as well as that mysterious "value" we keep talking about.

So, let's start there… let's demystify the concept of value.

Defining Your
Company's Value

Some years ago, I was visiting with one of my friends who, at the time, owned a very successful auto dealership. We got on the subject of marketing and he said that today, we are "over-supplied." The marketplace has become one, big homogenized glob of look-alike products. To his point—we have too many everything... too many automobile dealers, too many department stores, too many gift stores and too many places to purchase running shoes. Incidentally, he also said we had too many lawyers. Imagine my surprise!

But the more I thought about it, the more I realized he was right. And this creates serious challenges for those vying for consumer attention. The internet was supposed to expose us to volumes of information to help make buying decisions easier. Instead it has just made things more confusing for the consumers, and certainly harder for many businesses to get noticed.

And having endured one of our nation's most serious recessions, consumers are all the more careful with their spending. So, if you want to get people to buy your "widget," there has to be something about your widget that your prospects can't find anywhere else and simply can't do without.

Put simply, "sameness" will kill your company.

Your company's value, then, is what makes it unique. It is the collection of features and benefits that makes buying from your company better than buying from the others. So far, so good you say, but how exactly do we determine what that is?

The answer to that question lies in your vision statement.

FROM VISION TO VALUE

When you crafted your vision statement, you created a very broad statement to explain what you want your firm to look like, to achieve and why. To turn that concept into a value statement, you need to figure out how your vision benefits your customers.

Also called a Unique Selling Proposition or "USP," your value statement is a proposition statement that explains what makes you different. Federal Express uses "When it absolutely, positively has to be there overnight." Domino's Pizza guaranteed their delivery with "30 minutes or your money back."

Both of these USPs get right to the point, don't they? And you're immediately clear on what each of these companies has to offer. Someone wanting to ensure that their package was delivered on time would know that Fed Ex takes shipping overnight seriously. Likewise, someone who doesn't want to wait for their pizza could rest easy because if Domino's doesn't deliver within 30 minutes, their pizza will be free.

Your value proposition statement should do the same thing.

If your company manufactures auto parts, then ask yourself what makes those parts better than those from your competitor. Do you guarantee price? Do you guarantee it's in stock? What sets you apart from every other auto parts dealer on the web? Grab a paper and pen and make a list, then see which items stand out the most.

Now, you'll notice that our two example USPs don't say anything specifically about service or quality... and neither should you.

In fact, we need to be clear on what qualifies as uniqueness. Webster defines unique as "...the only one..." That's a high hurdle and eliminates many standards companies often use. For example, everyone offers great quality, great service and industry expertise and even if they don't really have it, they'll still say that they do. So, if these three items were on your list, you can mark them off... there's no uniqueness there. To find your USP or, as

Jaynie Smith calls it, your "Competitive Advantage," you're going to have to dig a little deeper.

So, let the work begin.

Start with that list of benefits you made and then keep going. Don't be afraid to look at other companies for inspiration. And if you're having trouble crafting a complete USP, try to first focus in on the positive aspects of your product or service. How is it useful? Why do people need it? How does it make life better? How do you make it different? How are your ingredients different? How do you deliver it differently? How do you service it or your customers differently? How do you assure quality difference? How do your customers experience the buying utilization differently? See if you can quantify the answer to these questions. If you do, you are making progress! Keep asking questions until you start coming up with adjectives and then start making your list.

Energizer, for example, touts their durability with "it keeps going and going and going." Nike went for inspirational with "just do it" while Maytag zeroed in on their reliability with "Maytag: The dependability people." Those are tag lines more than USPs, but they highlight longer lasting action and reliability as to what makes them different from everyone else.

Also remember that it doesn't matter if other people do what you do... what matters is if you're the first to announce it to the world.

I remember attending a long, two-day workshop by Jay Abraham a few years ago. He told a story about a beer company working with a marketing consultant to help craft their own USP. The consultant asked about the process the company used to make its beer and in their response, the beer executives mentioned that they used water from an artesian well.

"That's it," said the marketing consultant, but the executives didn't see it because many beer companies used that kind of water. "That may be true," the consultant replied, "but you'll be the first to describe it in your marketing campaign."

This advantage of being "first" can often be the uniqueness you're looking for. Our law firm uses fixed fee pricing when designing and creating estate plans. Other firms in our marketplace do the same thing, but we were the first—and still the only firm, by the way—to declare it publicly in our marketing.

We also complete plans for our clients within 30 days. There may be other firms that offer that same service. We offer a money-back guarantee if the client is not 100% satisfied with our work. Other firms might do that as well... but we proclaim it to the world. And that's what makes us different.

We proclaim these aspects of our business because we know that these issues are important to our clients. When choosing an attorney to create an estate plan, they're concerned with how much time it will take, how much money it will cost and how they can be sure they're really getting the best business or estate plan they can get.

We put those issues to rest by addressing them in our USP... and it's one of the reasons we're successful today.

Use this same process to analyze your business. Think of every step in your manufacturing, sales or service process. Which ones matter most to your clients? Which issues or concerns can you put to rest? Describe them in the context of a unique statement and you're on your way to creating your own USP.

Don't worry if you don't come up with something right off the bat—this isn't an easy task and between me and you, that's exactly why most business owners don't do it.

But easy or not, it's critically important work and once you've created your USP, it will become your company's mantra. Include your staff in the process, especially those who work closely with prospects and clients. Create teams and sponsor a contest... offer incentives... get client feedback.

But get started now.

Everyone in your organization should be able to describe your company's unique selling proposition to the marketplace and when they can, it will give your company focus and clarity about what you're trying to accomplish... other than just making a boat-load of money.

This statement will eventually lead to your tag line—that little one-liner catch phrase that embodies your company and its primary purpose. So, make it memorable. Create something that entices your prospects and inspires your staff.

And then use it anywhere and everywhere you can.

Now, your USP is a key component of a successful marketing campaign, but it's not the only component that needs your attention. In addition to understanding your company's value, you also need to understand the client you want to attract.

That is, you need to figure out *who* you're marketing to... and to do that, there are a few more questions that need to be answered.

IDENTIFYING YOUR
TARGET AUDIENCE

O ne of the biggest mistakes companies often make is failing to identify their ideal target audience. And while you might not consider yourself a "marketer," for purposes of this chapter that's exactly what you are.

Identifying your ideal target audience allows you to fine-tune your marketing message and thus increase your chances of reaching those prospects. Without this step, you're just shooting in the dark and you'll end up expending more time and effort but with dramatically dismal results.

And there's a simple reason for this:

When you don't identify your ideal audience, the alternative is to market to "everyone." And in theory, that might actually sound like a good plan. After all, why not try to appeal to anyone that might want your service or product? Wouldn't you have better sales if your audience wasn't limited to certain demographics?

Unfortunately, this plan will bring you more headaches than profit. Without a targeted audience, you can't have a targeted message and you won't be able to build the relationships that will benefit the prospect or your company the most. Drilling down your audience allows you to zero in on buying habits, preferences and concerns that affect a single group of consumers—consumers that are the most likely to buy from you.

So, exactly how much segmenting do you need to do?

There are actually a number of different questions you should try to answer about your audience.

So, let's start with the easiest question first: who buys from you now? Take a look at your current customer base and see what demographics are being represented. Do you see a trend in income, gender or marital status? What about geographic location or education? Breaking down your current clientele allows you to pinpoint who is most attracted to your product or service right now, and unless you're planning on making any drastic changes, that same demographic is who will be most likely to continue buying.

What if you don't have this kind of data on your customers?

Surprisingly, many businesses don't collect this type of information and have very little knowledge about who their customers really are. As a result, they have trouble tailoring their marketing message because they don't understand who it is they're trying to attract.

If this is your problem, not to worry—we're going to cover how to build a database that will provide you with everything you need to know about your existing customers as well as your prospects. But before we get to that, let's look at a couple of other tips that will help you identify your target market.

ANALYZE YOUR PRODUCT

Consumers buy for one of two reasons: to satisfy a need or to satisfy a want. Knowing which category your product or service falls into will help you identify your audience.

But this isn't always an easy distinction to make. Both needs and wants can help your market solve a problem, for example. Both can ensure your consumer's continued existence and even improve it in some cases. Wants can sometimes become so essential that they appear to be needs and likewise, a need can sometimes be delayed as if it were a want, without any serious consequence.

Meaning that it's up to you to decide how you want to portray your service.

To do this, start by creating a list of features for each product or service, and then outline the benefits that each of these features provide. Are these benefits that certain people can't live without? If so, you've found a primary niche. Could these features be translated into benefits that drastically improve the way someone does business or travels or raises their kids? That's another niche.

And understanding the people that make up these niches is the first step to identifying your target audience.

LOOK TO YOUR COMPETITION

Your competition has earned that title for a reason: they're competing with you for business. So, look at who they're targeting.

Do their advertisements seem to cater to women more than men? Are they appealing to a younger crowd or an older population? If they offer products or services similar to yours, what benefits do they tout and who would appreciate those benefits the most?

Then look at who they're not targeting. Is there an opportunity or a niche that you can capitalize on? A department store, for example, caters to a very specific market. They sell suits or shoes or beauty products and their market is very unique as a result. Wal-Mart, on the other hand, caters to the shopper who doesn't have time to go from store to store and needs to buy a variety of items—from clothing to groceries, liquor to automotive supplies in one-stop-shopping fashion. Now, consider a convenience store. They've drilled down the Wal-Mart philosophy even further and cater to the nearby consumer who's in a rush and doesn't want a full-blown shopping experience... they just need to pick up a gallon of milk or a quart of oil . . . that's why it's called a "convenience" store.

Each of these companies offer a similar set of products but each caters to a very unique and definable market. As a result, they're able to estimate variables such as net worth, social status, family status and geographic location. This information then helps them set prices, choose products and formulate a successful marketing plan.

So, now that you know the "what" and "who," let's talk about how you'll actually make the sale.

YOUR BASIC
MARKETING BLUEPRINT

S ay the word "marketing" and most business owners equate it with advertising; but these are two separate animals actually.

Advertising is the process of putting your company "out there"... think television commercials, billboard signs on the highway and ads in the yellow pages or a trade magazine and you'll be on the right track.

With advertising, you have no way to control who sees your ad nor do you have a proven method of measuring its effectiveness. Its sole purpose is to promote your company to the general public and if you're lucky, you might get a few new customers for your effort.

Now, that's not to say that advertising isn't worthwhile. Quite the contrary, advertising can do wonders for building brand awareness on a massive scale. It's the perfect place for a catchy tag line or your full USP we talked about earlier. Because of its format, it gives you the ability to take advantage of emotional hot points.

Marketing, on the other hand, is a systematic and strategic plan of lead generating activities that goes beyond general advertising and instead looks to target specific groups of consumers with specific, relevant messages.

Within a marketing strategy, you'll have research, support, distribution and a whole host of other components created to ensure that you're getting the best return on your investment.

Marketing uses advertising as one of these components, but then goes several steps further to see that the sale is made. Think of it this way: your marketing plan is the entire, multi-course meal. Advertising is simply the appetizer.

INBOUND VS. OUTBOUND

Now, it wasn't long ago that marketing followed much the same strategy as advertising. It was invasive, massive and basically hit-and-miss. Marketing meant reaching out to consumers in the hopes that they might be interested in buying, and if they weren't, you didn't waste time, moving on to the next possible sale.

Because of this mentality, marketing was a numbers game. The more people you contacted, the more chance you had for making a sale.

This strategy is now known as *outbound marketing*. It assumes that the effort to contact is made from the company, to the consumer. Of course, in order for this strategy to work, marketers had to be very aggressive and the result is the ad-ridden environment we live in today.

It wasn't long before consumers grew tired of all the junk mail, the cold calls and commercial-heavy television programming. So, they responded with DVRs that skip commercials, caller ID for their phones and spam filters for their email.

As a result, most of those outbound marketing messages weren't even getting through anymore, and marketers realized that something would have to change.

And then something did.

Inbound Marketing

With the Cone of Silence standing firmly around their targeted audiences, marketers knew they'd have to rethink their approach. This forced them to look at marketing from a different perspective and it wasn't long before marketing gurus such as Dan Kennedy, Seth Godin and HubSpot's Brian Halligan realized that the solution wasn't finding another way in… it was finding a way to draw your prospects out.

What if, they pondered, *there was a way to get prospects to raise their hand? What if, instead of bringing the product to the client, we could bring the client to the product?*

And inbound marketing was born.

Also often referred to as **relationship marketing** and **permission marketing**, inbound marketing still uses many of the same tools and mediums you know and love—it just changes the way you approach your market.

Where traditional outbound marketing was invasive and required you to bombard your audience with advertising to get the best results, inbound marketing instead works to position your company as the "expert"... the "go-to-business" for solutions in your particular industry.

And here's why it works:

When today's consumer is presented with a need or a dilemma, their first instinct is to seek out information.

They want to know if anyone else has had this problem or used this particular product. What options are available and how do they compare? What's the upside if they buy? And what's the downside if they don't?

They'll look at price to be sure, but they're actually more concerned with *value*... they want to know if this product or service does the best job of solving their problem or meeting their need.

Companies that can provide answers to these questions are seen as a valuable resource. The consumer feels educated about the topic and when they do decide to purchase, they do it because they feel they've made the best decision possible based on the information they've learned.

And who do you suppose they purchase from? That's right—the company that proved to be most useful in their research.

Let's get this out of the way now in the interest of space: if you compete on price, you are doomed; or at least destined to struggle and underachieve. I challenge you to be better than that.

For this reason, all the strategies and tactics that follow in this section are built around the concept of inbound marketing, and you'll find that this gives you a solid foundation to use for your own marketing campaign. But there's one caveat:

The marketplace is still changing. Turbulence reigns. Just as social media marketing was unheard of a few years ago, you can bet that new platforms and tools lie just over the horizon. So, by all means use this section of the book to get you started . . . but don't treat it as the ultimate marketing authority.

Because what works today may not work tomorrow... and who knows where we'll be further down the road. Successful marketing, like success in general, depends on your ability to adapt. Learn to go with the flow, and you'll be successful. Fight it and . . . . well, I'm sure you can imagine the outcome.

So, now that we've covered the big picture of marketing, let's talk about how to bring it all together.

MESSAGE-MEDIA-MARKET MATCH

One of the sacred concepts Dan Kennedy has taught followers for decades is the importance of creating a Message-Media-Market match in our marketing initiatives. To the un-initiated this means that you always structure your marketing message to precisely satisfy the hunger and interests of your target audience and use their preferred media to deliver it. This is a powerful concept that is the foundation for our entire marketing campaigns.

The lesson we miss is that we limit the M-M-M concept to marketing campaigns directed at our clients or prospects. To illustrate, here's an example of a stupid mistake I made.

Research on this book included interviews with a number of successful business owners and/or CEOs to get their input on a number of the covered topics. Their insights were incredible!

I wanted to say "Thank You" to those who helped and do so in a special way. One idea was to send a gift package from Shari's Berries. So we chose a very appealing, tasty package of chocolate covered strawberries and small, round, delectable cheesecakes. Yum!

I was so happy to cross that off my lengthy "to do" list and merrily went about my business. Two mornings later, I almost fell off the treadmill when I realized what I'd done.

Having made a blanket choice, I sent this wonderful sugar-filled Thank You package to Dan Kennedy. He's a diabetic! And, he happened to be one of the participants whose contribution I treasured the most.

How stupid is that? I clearly failed that Message-Media-Market test with that campaign. Efforts to rectify notwithstanding—and he was very gracious—I'm sure the first impression had a greater impact than the second.

The point is, Dan's Message-Media-Market match concept applies to all communication…to every outreach initiative, not just to clients and prospect marketing campaigns. It applies to employees and other centers of influence we seek to reach. Commit to this magic formula for every piece of communication that leaves your office. You'll get better results and avoid having chocolate covered strawberries on your face.

MAPPING YOUR SALES FUNNEL

A marketing campaign can include a variety of strategies and tactics, and these may differ from one campaign to the next as you target different demographics or promote different products. But regardless of which strategies and tactics you might use, they all have the same primary purpose: to generate qualified prospects who become part of a growing customer base.

To do this, you'll use a process known as a **Sales Funnel.**

Your sales funnel represents the big picture of your marketing plan and will define the tactics and strategies you choose to implement in a given campaign. So let's look at how a basic funnel works:

The top of the funnel represents the whole of your target market… that is, everyone that falls within your targeted group of prospects. These prospects haven't been proven as leads… in fact, you don't even know for sure that they want your product or service yet. The only thing you do know is that they fit within your targeted segment of buyers.

The bottom of your funnel represents the customers who, many steps later, proved to be qualified prospects that you were able to convert into paying clients.

Of course, it's the steps in between that will transform those unqualified prospects into the true-blue paying clients you're looking for, so let's go through these steps one by one:

The Offer:

The first thing your sales funnel needs to do is identify the prospects within your target market that are interested in what you're selling. And to do this, you need an offer.

Now, an offer can be just about anything. A clothing store might offer discounts on out-of-season merchandise, for example, or it might choose to apply a flat rate discount to the entire inventory. A restaurant might offer exclusive menu items for a special limited-time-only rate, or it could offer a selection of "value" items on the menu that never expires. Professional service businesses might offer a free consultation to new clients or a flat-rate "package" that allows customers to purchase popular services together in a single bundle.

And the list goes on and on.

Which offer is right for you will of course depend upon a number of variables, including your industry, your particular product and the market you're targeting, but regardless of these variables, your offer has one primary purpose: to get your prospects to "raise their hand."

And because different offers will attract different prospects, you'll need to do a bit of segmenting within your niche.

After all, your target market will consist of both prospects who are interested in buying now as well as those who like your service but aren't quite ready to make a purchase. Obviously you'll want to accommodate both groups, so you'll need a different offer for each.

And here's how that works:

In our law firm, we offer flat-fee estate plans delivered to the client within 30 days' time. This offer works great for those who already understand their options and know what they want from an estate plan. But we also want to connect with prospects who are interested in our service but aren't quite sure about the different options available to them, or aren't quite ready to get started with the planning process.

So, we offer a variety of free reports, videos and articles to help them learn more about the planning process and the various concerns that each planning option addresses. In exchange for access to this information, we ask these prospects to subscribe to our mailing list. This allows us to stay connected and "lead" these prospects further into our sales funnel.

Now, regardless of whom you're targeting or what you're selling, your offer should have a clear call to action, or "CTA." You want your prospects to click a link for example, fill out a form, answer a survey, register for a seminar or purchase a product… whatever it is, you have to clearly tell your prospects what it is you want them to do and you have to give them something in return.

Examples of solid CTA offers include:

- An invitation to attend a free webinar or seminar
- A free e-book
- A free report
- A free trial offer
- A free consultation
- Free access to members-only content or services
- An exclusive discount
- A free newsletter subscription
- Free training
- Free upgrades

Are you noticing how most of these options contain the word "free"? That's because inbound marketing requires you to give in order to get. In fact, the more compelling your free offer is, the more it hits the bull's eye for your target audience, and the more business you'll ultimately generate.

The other important thing to remember about creating a call to action is that it has to be simple, meaning your prospects should have no doubt about what to do next. "Click here to get your free report!" for example, or, "Sign up now for an exclusive discount!" are both good CTAs. Your job here is to direct your audience... tell them exactly what to do and how.

And if they do it, you've converted that prospect into a lead.

Lead Nurturing

Once you've acquired a lead, you'll want your sales funnel to be ready to nurture that relationship and move the prospect toward a conversion opportunity. Someone who subscribes to our mailing list, for example, receives regular communications in the form of newsletters, business and estate planning updates and targeted emails that keep our firm in front of our audience and remind them of the importance of having a solid plan. We also offer free consultations and seminars as part of our service and if they respond to that offer, they begin receiving a different set of targeted emails and publications.

This kind of nurturing strategy allows us to establish our firm as a valuable resource to our prospects... a resource that they'll turn to when they're ready to move forward. This kind of relationship is crucial to the success of your business and essential if you want to convert your prospects into paying customers.

Lead nurturing most commonly utilizes a type of email marketing called *autoresponders*. These autoresponders are specific content emails that are pre-written and set up to go out automatically on a certain schedule.

For example, you might send the first autoresponder out immediately after a new prospect subscribes to your mailing list. This autoresponder could welcome them to your list and give them a quick rundown of how to get the most from your company and/or its website. Another autoresponder could then go out a few days later, offering a free report. There are multiple steps to the process, each one creating a stronger relationship with the prospect.

Conversion and Sales

Now, the nurturing phase isn't over just because a prospect decides to buy. Quite the contrary, your customers are your "lowest hanging fruit" and should be treated as the gold that they are because in terms of "raising their hand," this group raised it the highest.

Dan Kennedy and Bill Glazer point out that most businesses want a customer to make a sale. They believe you want a sale to get a customer, one with whom you can make multiple sales over a long period of time.

In our law firm, those that choose to buy the business, estate or elder plan program continue to receive regular communications from us just like they did when they were still prospects. We keep these clients apprised of any new laws that might affect their plans and we offer regular reviews to ensure that their plans stay up-to-date and include changes in their finances and family status.

This process not only keeps the firm and our services in front of our targeted prospects, but also reinforces the relationships we have with our current clients, ensuring that they'll think of us first when they're ready to update or add new components to their plan or refer others like themselves to us.

Your sales funnel should include a similar system, allowing you to reach out and touch your customer base on a regular basis while incorporating new clients into your system at the same time.

Think of the tiers in your sales funnel as different levels of "membership"… the higher the level, the more benefits the member receives. So those at the top of your funnel should be able to see not only the benefits you provide to them but also the benefits they'll receive as they increase their level of membership. Those at the bottom of the funnel—your client base—should always be receiving the highest level of attention from your company. Kennedy refers to this as "building a fence around your herd."

Ironically, many companies do just the opposite. I've been working with a certain firm for nearly 30 years. They've never taken one step to strengthen the relationship I have with them. In fact, when I heard about other firms offering services of interest to me, I had to solicit them. Even after our meeting to discuss the program, I had to follow up with them to discover details about pricing and other terms. Businesses like this survive despite themselves. Surely, you aspire for more.

How often do you see deals advertised exclusively for new customers, while old customers get no extra perks at all? Some of the bigger cell phone companies are a good example, providing lower rates and deep discounts on merchandise to attract new customers but failing to provide the same benefits to the customers they already have. It's happened to me in dealing with T-Mobile for 10 years. I now use Verizon.

Of course, many of those existing customers may stick around for a while longer, often because they're tied into long-term service contracts, but you can bet that when those contracts expire, they won't hesitate to take their business elsewhere if a better deal comes along. Just like I did.

Your sales funnel ensures that not only do you have a system for converting leads into clients, but also that you have a plan for keeping those clients loyal and content… and ultimately, keeping your client base happy is a big step to surviving turbulent economic times.

So, now that you understand your funnel, let's look at how you're going to fill it with clients.

FILLING YOUR
MARKETING TOOLBOX

We've already established that the top of the funnel represents the whole of your target market... that is, everyone that falls within your targeted group of prospects. These prospects haven't been proven as leads and it's your job to find a way to get your prospects to raise their hand.

And this is where all those strategies and tactics come into play.

A couple of important points. As Bill Glazer says, "Don't fall for the excuse, 'But, Bill, my business is different.' Wise up . . . it's not." Second, remember if you cannot measure the results from your marketing, you should re-evaluate continuing its use. In today's turbulent business environment, you cannot afford to be guessing which marketing campaign is effective. You have to measure and know for sure.

Now, we're not going to cover each and every marketing strategy in-depth here... there are literally tons of books and websites out there that do that already and ultimately, that's not really the purpose of this book. When we work with our coaching and consulting clients, we help them develop and implement comprehensive marketing strategies that are customized to fit each client's unique set of needs and goals.

Obviously, we can't provide that depth here. But what we can do is cover some tactics that will help you stand out from the crowd by expanding your marketing efforts when everyone else is cutting back in the face of turbulence and uncertainty. Marketing, after all, is the lifeblood of your company's growth, even its very existence. And showing you how to grow your company in the face of turbulence is most definitely the purpose of this book.

Marketing can be broken down into two basic categories: offline and online. Both have their own set of pros and cons and both can be effective at bringing clients to your door. But you'll find that the best results come when you combine the two tactics and allow them to complement each other within your marketing campaign.

But before we get to that strategy, let's look at some of the tools you'll want to use:

ONLINE MARKETING

Online marketing is the fair-haired strategy in the Information Age. It offers a seemingly endless supply of tactics and strategies to choose from. Yet, many companies are still shying away from the online arena… they simply have no idea where to start.

In addition, many of the popular online marketing strategies are fairly time-intensive and somewhat difficult to measure in terms of ROI, so it's no surprise that entire industries are still resisting the digital era.

But despite all the obstacles, the internet is most certainly a place where your company needs a strong presence. Remember 90% of the population considers the search engines to be the most reliable way to find new products and services… which means that the only question is will they find you or your competition first?

Now, again, we're not here to explain how to launch a full-blown marketing campaign online, but we do want to touch on some strategies that you absolutely should be doing… regardless of market or industry.

Website

It's a given that every company, no matter how big or how small, should have a website. But what you may not realize is that those old, static websites from the past are no longer effective. There was a time when having a web presence was the equivalent of putting your company's brochure online, but this doesn't work anymore so if that's your plan… don't bother.

Instead, your website needs to be engaging, dynamic and *interactive*. Think of your website as your base of operations on the internet—it should serve as a portal to all of your services and products as well as act as a virtual storefront for your company.

That means that in addition to finding information about your company and its offerings, visitors to your site should also be able to find new content to read on a regular basis and have the ability to interact with your website in a number of different ways.

Blog

For starters, your website needs a **blog**. Short for "weblog," a blog is a collection of articles, called "posts" that readers can sort by date, topic and keyword. Blogs also give you the option of allowing your readers to comment on your posts, creating a way for your company to connect with your target market.

And connect you will.

Studies show that **companies that blog average 55% more website visitors than their non-blogging counterparts**.

In addition, **B2C (business-to-consumer) companies that blog regularly generate 88% more leads per month**, while **B2B (business-to-business) companies that blog generate 67% more leads per month** than companies that don't. [3]

Blog posts can include everything from staffing announcements to upcoming sales, but the real benefit of having a blog is using it to convey your value to your prospects. Successful business blogs include educational posts that cover a variety of concerns and issues common in the respective industry. A realtor's blog, for example, might include posts about the state of the housing market as well as articles that cover tips for selling your house, decorating ideas and energy-saving techniques.

A construction company's blog, on the other hand, could post updates about remodeling projects they're working on as well as home improvement ideas and how-to articles for do-it-yourself enthusiasts.

3　HubSpot, State of Inbound Marketing Lead Generation Report, 2010

WordPress is the most popular blogging platform and will give you the greatest amount of flexibility to integrate your blog into your existing website. Your blog should be updated regularly—at least once or twice a week—and you should include pictures and videos whenever possible.

Subscription Options

Your website also needs a way for visitors to subscribe, so that they're alerted when new updates are posted. This also allows you to build a mailing list of interested prospects that you can use in more targeted marketing campaigns.

There are two ways to provide this subscription option and you should take advantage of both:

The first is what's known as an **RSS feed** and if you have a blog, you have RSS. For WordPress users, your feed is usually located at www.yoursitesname.com/feed/, but you can easily locate your feed (regardless of blogging platform) by using a "feed management service" such as FeedBurner, FeedBlitz and MailChimp.

The second method is to offer an **email subscription** option and this is where you start building that all-important mailing list we've been talking about. The easiest way to do this is to sign up with one of the many mailing management services on the internet—Aweber, InfusionSoft, iContact and MailChimp are all good options.

When you sign up for one of these programs, you can create "lists" within your account, allowing you to segment your audience by a variety of filters and interests (don't worry—we're going to cover this in more detail in just a bit). The management service also provides you the code you need to insert a contact capture form on your website. The data collected through this form is stored on the management service's web server for easy access.

Contact Information

One of the biggest ways to frustrate a potential prospect is to make it difficult to find out how to contact you directly or limit their options for seeking assistance. Bury your phone number or force visitors to use a web form as their sole means of contact and you can bet they'll go looking somewhere else for their solution.

Instead, include your company's address and phone number on every page of your website. Also include a collection of Frequently Asked Questions (FAQs), a sitemap and an email option for support as well. The more accessible and helpful your company is on the internet, the more credible you'll appear to your market.

Landing Pages

If your website is the virtual storefront, then think of landing pages as the doorway to different departments. Landing pages are independent, stand-alone pages that focus on a specific concern or niche and contain an equally specific call to action.

For example, my estate planning law firm has a landing page that targets consumers going through probate and another page for those interested in learning more about living trusts. I also have a page dedicated to wills and yet another for trust administration. Each landing page offers a free report on the topic in question in exchange for the visitor's contact information.

These pages allow me to determine who within my target market needs probate services versus those interested in more general estate planning options, and, as a result, I can create targeted marketing campaigns for each group.

Search Engine Optimization

Also called "SEO," search engine optimization is the process of making your website and other online content search-engine-friendly so that you'll rank well in the search results.

This process is comprised of a variety of tactics that include keyword research and placement, meta tag optimization, content creation and backlink building. This is a simplified list, of course, so if you want to get serious about SEO (and you should), you'll need to either do some in-depth research or hire a professional because it's a fairly complex and time-consuming process.

But as time-consuming as it might be, it's definitely worth the effort and here's why:

Those 90% that see the search engines as their primary resource for finding new products and services are very particular about the links they choose to click. In fact, 60% of those clicks go to the top three organic results, meaning that your paid links aren't getting the attention you thought. In fact, paid links only receive 25% of the total clicks. [4]

It also means that if you're not one of those top three listings on page one, you're missing out on quite a bit of website traffic, since 75% of users never click past page one at all. [5]

And this is where SEO comes into play.

Research shows that companies that blog, for example, have 434% more pages indexed by Google and 97% more inbound links [6]—two crucial components to improving your rankings in the search engines.

Add to that the effects of smart keyword placement and other SEO tactics, and you begin to see the importance of adding SEO to your overall marketing strategy.

Now, you'll notice that I said to use SEO for your websites and *other online content*. That's because the benefits of SEO aren't limited to traditional websites. Google and the other search engines index a variety of online content, including videos, landing pages and even some of your social media profiles. Granted, you won't have much control over how these third-party sites approach SEO, but if you're given the opportunity to choose keywords and/or add custom content about your company to a profile or page out on the web, do so... at the very least, you'll benefit from the additional inbound link and you'll also be improving your overall visibility.

Video Marketing

In the world of internet marketing, video is the next big thing and it gained that status for one simple reason: Google loves it. Do a search on Google and you'll find that videos rank in the top spots on page one every single time.

Now, does this have anything to do with the fact that Google owns YouTube? Perhaps... but it's also because most users prefer to watch a video in lieu of reading copy.

The average internet user watched approximately 23.2 hours of video for the month of December, 2011, for a national total of 43.5 billion videos. Mobile video streaming has increased by 93% worldwide (35% in the U.S.)

---

4   MarketingSherpa, February 2007
5   MarketShare.Hitslink.com, October 2010
6   HubSpot, State of Inbound Marketing Lead Generation Report, 2010

from 2010 to 2011 and experts estimate that mobile video services will generate a whopping $30 billion in revenues by 2017 [7].

Clearly, video has captured the attention of your target market... the question is, are you going to take advantage of that captive audience?

Now, assuming your answer is yes, the good news is that video is fairly easy to create and you have options in the way you produce it.

Videos can be nothing more than you on screen, walking your audience through a particular topic. You can also create videos that use slide shows for the visual portion while you narrate. If slide shows are a bit too plain for you, there are plenty of services and software packages out there that will create some eye-catching animation to illustrate your audio.

Your videos don't have to be long—in fact, 2 to 3 minutes is considered ideal—and you can use videos in a number of different ways. An introduction video on your home page is always a good idea and you can turn any of those blog posts you're creating into a short video as well. You can use video to launch a new product, announce a new service or just cover a topic that relates to your industry, making video a marketing tool you simply can't do without.

Email Marketing

Email marketing is, of course, about connecting with your audience via email, and there are a number of ways you can utilize this tool. Since we mentioned using autoresponders earlier in this section, we'll start there.

Autoresponders

Autoresponders are basically automated messages that are sent via email to your list on a predetermined schedule. Like video, autoresponders can be used in a number of different ways. You can use them as a general way to stay in touch with your list, for example, or you can give your autoresponders a more specific purpose and use them to drive traffic, generate sales or attract new leads.

And I'll give you an example of both scenarios:

Mike Dooley, entrepreneur and author the New York Times bestseller, *Infinite Possibilities: The Art of Living Your Dreams*, operates a website called The Adventurer's Club (www.tut.com). As a subscriber, you'll receive an

---

7   DaCast.com, January 2012

email every three or four days with a short, inspirational message. Mike calls these emails "Notes from the Universe" and gives you the ability to personalize your messages by including a few goals in the sign up process. These goals, along with your contact information, go into Mike's mailing list and the autoresponders begin. The result is that you receive regular, inspirational updates from his website without Mike having to worry about manually sending out mass emails every week.

Now, to demonstrate how you can use autoresponders for a more specific purpose, I'll use my law firm as an example. I have a landing page that targets consumers in need of probate assistance. When they sign up on this landing page, they receive a free report and immediately begin receiving an autoresponder series that encourages them to call our office and schedule a free consultation. Unlike the Notes from the Universe example above, this autoresponder series doesn't go on indefinitely. If the reader responds and sets up a consultation, they're removed from the autoresponder series and go into a different list. If, however, they don't request a consultation, the autoresponder series runs its course and then the prospect is placed into a general "stay in touch" mailing list.

As you can see, autoresponders can be utilized in multiple ways so it makes sense to think about the different scenarios that could result from your marketing campaign and then create autoresponders to address each one. Remember, the goal of inbound marketing is to create a relationship with your audience, keeping in mind that some will be ready to buy while others won't… using autoresponders to address the different needs of your audience will ensure that you connect with as many prospects as possible.

Digital Newsletters

Autoresponders aren't the only way to stay in front of your prospects. You can also use newsletters to touch base and remind your audience of the value you bring to the table.

Digital newsletters can include exclusive, original content as well as links to existing content on your website or elsewhere on the internet. You can also share news about your staff, updates about your company and information about upcoming sales, promotions and product launches.

The key to a successful newsletter is twofold: first, you have to be consistent. If your newsletter is monthly for example, then send one out each and every month. The quickest way to have your list grow "cold" is to email your prospects sporadically—they'll forget who you are and lose interest in what you have to say.

The second rule of a good newsletter is to keep your content interesting. Feel free to promote your products and services, but also include plenty of useful and informative content as well. The more engaging your newsletter is, the more successful it will be.

Social Media

Although social media is by far the most popular marketing tool on the internet, there are still plenty of CEOs and business owners that resist using it to promote their businesses.

And the reasons are valid.

Social media is time-consuming, requiring you to maintain an active and on-going presence in order to build any kind of real following. It can also be difficult to measure in terms of effectiveness and, at least for those just getting started, it can be utterly and totally overwhelming.

But despite these objections, social media remains one of the most powerful marketing tools available to you today. And here's why:

Regardless of how you might feel about social media, your target market has embraced it completely. According to a 2010 study by the Nielsen Company, internet users spend more time on blogs and social networks than they do on email... *three times more*, in fact, averaging 4.6 hours a week worldwide.

And all this usage translates into new business for savvy companies taking advantage of this resource. B2B marketers found that social media helps to increase page rank, improve organic SEO and influence keyword purchases, according to a BTOB Magazine study in 2010.

Of course, deciding how to use social media can be a little confusing, so let's quickly cover the top three platforms you should be focusing on:

Facebook

Facebook currently boasts more than 800 million users, making it big enough to be the third largest country in the world in terms of population. Those 800 million users spend a total of 8.3 billion hours a month, sharing more than 3.5 billion pieces of content each week.

To use Facebook you'll need to sign up and create a personal profile, but it's not your profile that's going to connect you to your target audience—it's your fan page.

This fan page is essentially a separate profile and one that can be customized to do all sorts of great marketing things. Your profile image for example—also called the "cover photo"—is 851 x 315 pixels in size, making this area prime real estate for your marketing message. Facebook does impose some rules about what can and cannot go into this area, but those rules notwithstanding, it's still a great visual tool to capture your audience's attention.

Like your profile, your fan page has a "wall" to compile all your posts as well as those from your fans and, using third party applications, you can also feed your blog and Twitter posts directly to your fan page's wall, so that your fans have immediate access to your other online profiles. In addition to these automated posts, you should also be posting exclusive content on a daily basis, whether it's to comment on someone else's status, give your thoughts on a current news item or update your audience on the various happenings within your company.

But the biggest feature your fan page offers is that it gives you the ability to add custom "tabs," creating sub-pages that can be designed to do just about anything you like.

To create these custom tabs, Facebook uses iFrames to "call" the coding for the custom page from a separate URL. This means that whatever you can do with a web page, you can probably accomplish on your fan page as well, such as embedding subscription signup boxes, videos, flash files and RSS feeds.

This gives you a huge amount of creative leeway with your fan page, allowing you to essentially create a mini-site within Facebook's framework and entice new visitors to "like" your page to access all your content.

Twitter

Twitter is a micro-blogging site that allows its users to communicate via "tweets"—that is, mini-posts of 140 characters or less. Twitter currently has over 100 million active users and experts estimate that this will grow to approximately 250 million users by the end of 2012.

Now, if you think the idea of "tweeting" sounds like a waste of time, consider this: According to a December, 2011, MediaBistro study, 34% of marketers have successfully generated new leads using Twitter and over 20% have actually closed deals via tweets.

And fortunately, getting started on Twitter is relatively easy.

In addition to uploading a profile image, you can also create a customized background image, but there's not a ton of marketing real estate to work with and there's no ability to embed any flash or scripting.

That means that the power of Twitter will come from the tweets you post rather than flashy graphics and applications.

Now, there is an art to successful tweeting.

If you use Twitter solely to promote your services and products, your followers will quickly tune you out. Some self-promotion is okay, but it should be filtered with an abundance of other, non-promotional tweets.

Which means you have to find something other than your services to tweet about.

Fortunately, Twitter offers an informal setting where just about anything goes. You can comment or reply to others' tweets, post quotes and sayings that you find inspirational or even just repost someone else's tweet because you like it (known as a retweet).

And retweeting is actually something you should strive for.

When your followers are retweeting your posts, that means that your content is getting seen by all their followers as well, and that's free publicity for you. So, what makes someone retweet a post?

According to a study by WhiteFire SEO, 92% of users retweet content because they find it interesting. 66% cited a personal connection and 32% did so because an incentive (there's those free offers again!) was involved.

And the power of having your posts retweeted is substantial: 55% of Twitter users said they found new people to follow because that user was mentioned or retweeted by someone they're already following. And since 79% of Twitter users recommend the brands they follow to others [8], it's crucial to ensure that your Twitter content goes viral.

---

8   Edison Research, 2010

LinkedIn

With all the fuss about Facebook and Twitter, it might seem that LinkedIn has been left in the dust, but that's all starting to change. Marketers are quickly realizing the power of an active LinkedIn profile, specifically when it comes to networking with other professionals and generating business for business-to-business companies.

According to HubSpot's 2011 State of Inbound Marketing Report, LinkedIn generated three times more referrals to B2B sites than Facebook and 61% of the conversions generated by social media for B2B's were courtesy of LinkedIn.

Those are substantial numbers for companies that sell primarily to other companies, but it also demonstrates the potential of establishing mutually-beneficial relationships with potential vendors.

Now, because LinkedIn is a "professional" social media platform, there's not much customizing to worry about. Instead, you have a personal profile to complete and you can also create a LinkedIn page for your company.

But it's the LinkedIn Groups that hold the real networking power. Once you've joined, you can post to these groups, commenting on existing discussions or starting new discussions of your own. LinkedIn members are very vocal and very active within their groups, so it's almost a sure-thing that you'll get at least a few responses back. In addition, members frequently browse the discussions and "connect" with those who appear to be active within the group and knowledgeable about their topic.

That makes LinkedIn a great way to connect with other professionals who could bring real value to your company.

OFFLINE MARKETING

Contrary to popular belief, offline marketing isn't dead. In fact, many of the tried and true tactics you learned about in Marketing 101 are still alive and well. Ignore them at your peril.

You just have to know how to use them.

Offline marketing is generally more expensive than its online counterparts and during turbulent times like these, every dollar counts.

This, of course, makes it difficult to splurge on the pricier offline options, such as TV commercials and mass mailings, which is why so many companies start pulling back their marketing efforts when times are tough—the return just doesn't justify the expense. But remember, many of these traditional strategies use the old, interruption marketing mindset... a mindset that we've already established no longer works.

Fortunately, those aren't your only offline options and in fact, there are some better (and more cost-effective) alternatives that will net you much better results in any economy.

Newsletters

If you accept the premise that you make a sale to gain a customer rather than get a customer to make a sale and that a customer brings value to your company through repeated purchases over a period of time, then you have to accept the notion that your relationship with that customer is critical... that a sale is almost incidental to the relationship. It also follows that if that relationship creates "raving fans," to pilfer from the title of Ken Blanchard's great book, it will lead to referrals.

Count me, alongside Dan Kennedy and others, as strong advocates of a newsletter as a way to nurture and strengthen the relationship with your customers. Yes, I'm talking about an old-fashioned, off-line, print on paper, delivered through the U.S. Postal service to your customer's mailbox, multi-page newsletter, in addition to the online version we mentioned earlier. I can hear the screeds and howling now. *How yesterday.* It takes work. I don't have time. I don't have that much to say. I can't afford it.

When wearing my attorney hat, counseling my business clients in the law firm about a new venture they are considering, I advise that if your deal doesn't have enough money to include great legal counsel and a great CPA, then you don't have a deal worth considering. Likewise, when wearing my consulting hat—coaching or developing marketing plans—I advise clients that if their marketing budget does not have enough money to support a permanent newsletter campaign they need to find more money for marketing.

Most commonly I see clients start a newsletter campaign and like a North Korean missile test, it fizzles shortly after take-off. So, there is not enough time taken to create the infrastructure around the effort. In other words, people fail to use a planning process—such as our Strategic Alignment process—to assure long-term success.

The downside to a newsletter effort is that it is difficult to measure the effectiveness of a newsletter campaign as a marketing strategy. And, you know how I feel about spending money on marketing efforts you cannot measure. The key point is that a newsletter can be a marketing campaign. It will help, as Dan Kennedy says, build a high fence around your herd of customers, keep them depending on you for food…product…service.

There are many reasons why newsletters fail. Spending the time and money to implement a consistent, exciting newsletter marketing campaign can pay big dividends for your business.

Direct Mail

There are books, treatises, seminars, newsletters, consultants and other material on direct mail available for your consumption and study. Here's how it became evident to me that direct mail can be a vital tool in your marketing toolbox.

When I started my estate planning law practice I used seminar marketing as the primary method of filling my sales funnel. We would offer educational workshops, offer a free consultation and invite people to come visit with us about their estate planning concerns in a free, no obligation consultation. It still works.

We used newspaper ads as our primary advertising strategy. We would spend thousands of dollars to place an ad in the paper. We could select the section of the paper it appeared in, but we could not get a guarantee where in the section it would appear. We wanted right page, above the fold, upper right hand location for best results. But what we got was left page, below the fold, lower right placement buried in some location where our ideal client never looked.

I started to realize we were spending thousands of dollars getting our message to people who did not care, had no interest and would not find our offer appealing. It was difficult to measure and to test specific elements of our ad. We could only assess whether we were attracting our ideal prospect after the fact. I wanted more precision in our marketing campaigns. Like everything else in a successful business, the guess-work had to go.

Then I started to discover direct mail. What appealed to me is that as a concept, it's pretty simple. You can target and you can measure. Having said that, direct mail is one of the most sophisticated, challenging marketing strategies you can implement.

It requires clarity of your target market. You have to have a great list and know where to find it. It requires expertise to take a list and refine it to come up with even higher quality prospects. It requires copywriting knowledge and that alone requires a library full of books and years of practice. It requires you have a solid, relational database to track results. It requires someone to manage the process. That expertise can, and should be, found. It's one of the reasons Notch It Up Strategies is in business.

Last week I was visiting with a friend, not yet a client, about his business and how he markets. He hasn't become a client yet because he has not yet qualified himself to be one. He still thinks he's in the *business of offering and servicing* a particular widget to the public. That may be what he does but that's not the business he's in. He's in the *business of marketing* that widget, and the corresponding services, to the public. When he gets that, and lets us help him, his revenue, and margins, will grow.

One point I helped him discover is that 80% of his customers come from within a radius of five miles from his stores. Yet, he budgets well into six figures on newspaper, television and yellow page ads. Do you think direct mail would help his business? If you answered "no," put the book down.

Obviously, he's starting to change the way he looks at his business and how he markets that business. He'll get there… and when he does, we'll help him grow.

Write a Book

There's no better way to show off your expertise than by pointing to the book you've written on that very topic. Granted, this kind of undertaking isn't one you should approach lightly and unless you're quite comfortable putting pen to paper, you may want to bring in a professional writer to help you out.

But those small cautions aside, writing a book gives you a chance to really showcase your knowledge and promote the vision that is your company.

Of course, to be effective, your book will need to relate to your business in some way. But that doesn't mean you can't get creative with your topic. If retail clothing is your industry for example, a book that covers all the different aspects of the fashion world would certainly be appropriate as would a book that explains what it takes to launch your own line of clothes.

Just remember, the key is to find a topic that appeals to your target audience. A book written for the average bank customer, for instance, will be much different than a book written for your wealthiest investors, so go back to the outline of your target market and figure out what would appeal to your prospects.

When you're ready to publish your book, you can use Amazon's Publish-On-Demand service to control printing costs and time the launch of your book to sync with your marketing campaign. And yes, in case you're wondering… that's one of the reasons I wrote this book when I did.

Go Local

Local advertising used to be the meat and potatoes of a good marketing campaign, but then the internet came along and everything went global. As a result, marketers seem to struggle with the concept of local advertising now, most likely because it seems counterintuitive to what they've become accustomed to doing on the World Wide Web. But local advertising is actually where offline methods can shine.

People do actually still use their local yellow pages for example, so you can start there. You can also get quite a bit of free publicity—yes, I said *free*—by writing an article or press release for a local newspaper or regional magazine. Local newspapers are also more interested in community events so the next time you host such a gala, use your local publications to promote it.

And speaking of local events, when was the last time your company was involved in one?

Sponsor a 5K, participate in a local trade show or even host your own open house or educational seminar. The more visible you are the more familiar and comfortable your company will feel to your prospects.

Give Away Your Goods

If you want to measure the strength of a company's sales, just look at the amount of free stuff they give away. It wasn't so long ago, for example, that banks were luring new customers in the door with free checking, free checks, free ATMs and free toasters for opening an account. It became so competitive, in fact, that those free accounts also started paying interest and signup bonuses just so the banks could add more "free stuff" to their list of benefits.

But as the economy began to tank, those freebies began to disappear and while you'll still find "free checking" offers, many of the extra perks that made the offer outstanding are now long gone.

Ironically, this is exactly when you should be giving away some things for free, because as the economy gets tougher, consumers are paying much more attention to finding the best deal. It's all about *value*, remember? And offering your prospects some free stuff on the side is always a great way to add value to your offer.

Fortunately, your list of giveaways doesn't have to break the bank to be effective.

For example, if you were to look through the collection of pens you have in your desk, how many have another company's name on them? There's a reason that all those little company-sponsored promotional items have been around for so many years… they work.

And the best part about this type of marketing is that it's very subtle. There's no hard-sell and there's no invasive action required on your part—the promotional item does the selling for you and is a powerful tool in creating brand recognition.

Of course, your list of giveaways isn't limited to pens and paperweights. Those free reports you created for your website and landing pages can easily be printed and given out to your local market as can your newsletter.

You can also create brochures, branded calendars and promotional rack cards that can be mailed out or even placed in a variety of public areas around town… your local library, for example, the Chamber of Commerce, grocery stores and even gas stations often allow local businesses to put out business cards or other, small promotional materials.

DEVISING YOUR STRATEGY

With your marketing tools in place, it's fairly easy to see how offline and online strategies can work together.

Use your website and social media profiles to promote an in-house sale or book launch, for example, or to provide registration for an upcoming seminar. Likewise, you can use your print marketing materials to promote a new webinar or downloadable report, or just invite your prospects to follow you on online.

And building this kind of active, engaging presence is what inbound marketing is really all about.

In the turbulence of extreme competition and information overload, your goal is to give your prospects multiple ways to find you and interact with your company. This presence creates a sense of familiarity and reliability... your company becomes the company that everyone knows and trusts, not because they've specifically done business with you in the past but because they see you everywhere they turn. You become a part of their community, both online and off and when they do start looking for the services or products you offer, you'll automatically be their first choice.

Capturing Information

Obviously in order to do this kind of targeted marketing, you'll want to capture as much information as possible about your audience and you'll likely use your mailing list management system we discussed earlier to do that.

But how much information is enough... or too much?

Unfortunately, there's no one right answer. Asking for your prospects' full bio the first time they subscribe to your electronic newsletter or blog is probably going to limit the number of people that subscribe. They don't mind giving you a first name and email in exchange for a free report, for example, but they'll be a little more skeptical about handing out their mailing address and phone number.

On the other hand, the more information you have about your audience, and the more you can slice-and-dice demographic and psychographic information about your prospects, the more effective your marketing will be. So, in addition to asking for basic contact information, you also want to gather data beyond basic demographics and capture things such as the industry they're in, the position they hold, the amount of money they make and the issues or concerns that led them to your website.

For example, the net worth of clients in a typical estate planning law firm will vary widely, ranging from modest amounts to billions. Those with a high net worth will be interested in messages that those with a more modest net worth will care nothing about. And the reverse is also true.

If we are advising a law firm on using changes in estate tax laws—currently a hot topic—in their marketing messages, we'll want to be able to deliver that message to those who have the greatest interest in the subject.

And that makes capturing and tracking the net worth of their clients and prospects critical to the success of this effort.

But before you can ask for this very personal and very private data, you'll first have to establish a solid rapport with your audience. And that's where all these relationship-building strategies come into play.

The more credible your presence is and the more value your audience believes you have, the more information you can successfully request.

To start out, you should just ask for basic subscription information—name and email should be sufficient—and in return, your new subscribers get access to your electronic newsletter and whatever free giveaway you've offered. They'll also receive your autoresponders, and this is where you can start encouraging them to open up and share their personal data with you.

You do this through the various offers you extend. An invitation to an exclusive, subscription-only webinar, for example, would be a good excuse to ask for more data. You could also invite your audience to complete a survey and ask for some of this information in your questionnaire.

Your objective is to build a solid database that reveals the needs and desires of your prospects, but you can't do that overnight.

Instead, choose your mailing list management software wisely and then use the inbound marketing tactics we've mentioned here to build trust with your audience. You'll find that your conversions are much higher and the data you collect is much more reliable.

Creating a Marketing Plan

In order to build a targeted marketing campaign like the one we're discussing here, you'll need a detailed marketing calendar to work from.

Every year, my law firm sits down in October to begin developing the calendar for the coming year and this exercise forces us to think about the messages we want to deliver as well as the services we want to focus on offering.

Of course, we want that calendar to reflect our overall marketing plan for the year, so it's important to have that in place first.

Your marketing plan starts with the basics of your company—your vision, your mission, your USP and of course, the niche markets you want to focus on.

It then outlines the general overview of your marketing campaigns—the services or products you want to target, the tools (assets) you'll use to do it and the methods you'll use to measure your results.

And here's how you do it. Start by asking some simple questions:

- What services or products generate the most sales with the highest margins?
- What new services or products (if any) are we planning to introduce in the coming year?
- What services or products do we want to focus on in the coming year?
- What marketing tools/campaigns have worked well for us in the past?
- What marketing tools/campaigns have failed to produce the results we wanted? Why?
- Has our target market changed in any way?
- How does our ideal client compare to our current client/prospect base?

Now, if this is a new venture, you may not have a good reference point for what works and what doesn't, but there are other ways to set goals, outline campaigns and measure performance.

One way is to research your competition. Pick the top five and look at what they do. How does their product or service compare to yours? What marketing tools do they tend to use the most?

You should also dig deeper into your particular niche. The same SCOT analysis you used to define your critical success factors can also be used to diagram your market and figure out where the best opportunities lie.

Your strengths, for example, would be the products or services that seem to be the "hottest" right now. And even if you've yet to make a single sale, it's still fairly easy to find out what consumers are buzzing about the most.

Your weaknesses would identify the areas where you struggle… are there drawbacks to your product or service that make you less competitive? Better to address that issue now rather than after you've launched a full-blown marketing campaign.

Your opportunities will tell you what areas or markets offer the biggest potential for growth and your threats will identify the areas where you'll have the most competition.

With this simple analysis, you now have a basic overview of your market and you're likely already thinking about how to flesh out the opportunities and protect your company from the related threats.

Also remember that your campaigns and goals may vary between the different products and services you sell. Because of that, creating a one-page marketing plan for each product or service you offer is a good way to get a handle on how your marketing campaigns will differ.

Wait a minute… one page?

Yes… one page. While the traditional marketing plan is typically an all-inclusive tome designed to cover every aspect of marketing and requiring extensive research and time to create, a concise one-page version can get you moving quickly in the right direction and toward the profits you seek. In fact, there are several marketing gurus that have touted the benefits of a one page marketing plan over the years and since each version has its own unique set of perks, I think it's beneficial to touch on some of the more popular ones here.

For example, Philip Kotler, International Marketing Professor at the Kellogg School of Management at Northwestern University and author of a variety of graduate-level textbooks on the subject of marketing, is the original creator of the four Ps of marketing—product, place, pricing and promotion. His one-page plan follows that line of thinking by compiling information on your objectives, your market, your offer, distribution, pricing and promotion into a single sheet of paper.

Read Jay Levinson's and Michael McLaughlin's *Guerilla Marketing* on the other hand, and you'll see a plan that incorporates some of Kotler's basics but also adds information to address how you'll reach your target market. This plan talks briefly about purpose, product and demographics but then really zeros in on the tools you'll use to promote and deliver your product to consumers.

And still yet another version by accomplished entrepreneur Nolan Bushnell is the brochure-style plan that literally maps out your product, your price and the benefits of buying. Think of this brochure, Bushnell says, as a design document for the rest of the company.[9] It includes a list of features for your engineering department, an outline of research that's needed and an overview of production so that you can measure the costs associated with your product.

The great thing about these different versions is that you can adapt them to suit your individual needs. Each one helps you focus on different areas of your marketing campaign and used in conjunction with one another, you'd end up with a fairly detailed marketing plan condensed in three sheets of paper.

And with a basic marketing plan complete, one that compliments the Strategic Plan we discussed earlier, you can start focusing on your calendar.

Creating Your Marketing Calendar

Your marketing calendar is literally an annual calendar that breaks down your various marketing activities month-by-month.

If your marketing plan includes social media, webinars and direct mail as your tools of choice, for instance, then you'd use your calendar to set deadlines for each of those milestones. This also allows you to see how the different components will work together and make any changes in process, tools or timeline if need be, to ensure your "launch" runs smoothly.

As an example, January might have you in design mode, creating a new fan page for Facebook and setting up profiles on your chosen social media platforms. You'll also need to determine who will create a direct mail piece (should you decide to offer one) and what exactly it will say.

If a webinar is the offer that drives prospects into your sales funnel, then your mail piece and fan page should both promote this event. Obviously you'll want to have a fairly good idea of what your webinar will include before designing the other promotional components.

This calendar also ensures that you meet your marketing milestones, making it easier to track your progress and evaluate performance, which brings us to the next piece of the marketing puzzle…

---

9   *The Power of a One-Page Marketing Plan*, Inc., July 31, 2009, http://www.inc.com/nolan-bushnell/2009/07/the_power_of_a_onepage_marketi.html

Measuring Your Results

Yes, I'm going to remind you of measuring again because it's so critical to profitable allocation of your marketing dollars. In order to measure the effectiveness of a marketing campaign, you must first understand what the results data represents.

An increase in sales, for example, doesn't automatically mean profit, especially if you're not clear on how much it costs your company to offer those new products or services. Likewise, more traffic to your website doesn't necessarily mean more prospects. You'll first need to compare page views with conversion rates for your call-to-action to determine if your triggers are working the way you had hoped.

And this kind of measuring is perhaps one of the most important components to successful marketing because, as we've said before, what works today isn't guaranteed to work tomorrow.

Remember the market is always changing and new trends and technology continue to emerge. Marketing your company successfully will require you to not only stay on top of those changes, but also learn how to use that knowledge to measure your own campaigns and make tweaks along the way.

How Much is Enough?

As you're outlining all the potential tools and resources you could use to promote your business, it's a given that cost will cross your mind.

After all, the reason that marketing is often the first casualty in a struggling economy is because, plain and simple, it's an expense. For most business owners, it's an expense that appears to be optional.

But the truth is, there's no such thing as "too much marketing"... especially in such turbulent times. Your company should be constantly looking for new ways to strengthen your brand, connect with your market and establish your business as the foremost authority in your niche. In fact, as marketing guru, Dan Kennedy, says, your goal should be to outspend your competition when acquiring new customers.

How you choose to accomplish this task is flexible and there are a number of ways that you can achieve your marketing goals without breaking the bank.

Now, it used to be that businesses spending anywhere from 5% to 10% of revenue on marketing could expect a reasonable return on their investment. But in today's market, that's no longer a guarantee. Not only is your competition more aggressive for business, there's also more competitors to worry about.

As a result, 10% may not be enough... especially if you're a new company venturing into a highly competitive market. On the other hand, 10% may be more than you need if you cater to a very select niche of people where there's little to no competition.

So, throwing all those "rules" out the window, let's start by asking the obvious question: how much do you have to spend?

How much can you truthfully afford to invest in marketing without putting your company in a bind? Does that amount allow for emergencies and other unexpected expenses?

This is really the starting point for your marketing budget and the number you come up with should be considered your ceiling, come hell or high water. If your company enjoys a sudden influx of cash later on in the year, you can reconsider that number and adjust accordingly. Likewise, if things suddenly go bad, you'll need to rethink your budget and perhaps shave that number a bit to meet your financial obligations.

Now, having an annual number is just half the battle because the key to effective marketing isn't necessarily how much you spend... it's how you spend it. Investing all your marketing dollars into a single television ad, for example, might generate some interest in your business but you're not going to see the same rate of return over time that you would have seen by splitting the money into smaller and more cost-effective, long-term campaigns.

And it's those cost-effective, long-term campaigns we're recommending here.

For instance, building your website may require a bit of cash up front, but once it's done, the on-going cost to maintain it is relatively low. Hosting can be had for less than $10 a month for example, and the average cost to renew your domain name is about $12 to $15 a year. All that content we suggested you create can be done in-house if you've got the right staff or you can outsource it to a freelancer on an hourly or per-piece basis. This flexibility allows you to keep a handle on your expenses and control exactly how much you'll need to spend each month.

Mailing list management services are another cheap way to build a high-impact marketing campaign. Some services offer a fairly impressive number of features for a relatively low price, ranging anywhere from $10 to $30 a month… there's even a few, like MailChimp, that offer free plans for clients with less than 500 subscribers. If you're just getting started and your marketing budget is small, this is a great alternative to some of the more expensive mailing list options.

In the offline marketing arena, you can focus on trade shows that are in town, for example, eliminating the added expenses for travel and hotel. Direct mail costs can be reduced by printing your own postcards and flyers or by joining forces with other small businesses in your area and doing a joint venture promotion. (Incidentally, joint ventures are a huge option online too—if you're looking for ways to get big exposure for minimal costs, joint ventures are the answer.)

And let's not forget the benefits of free publicity. Having your company mentioned in a local newspaper will do much more for your bottom line than that paid advertisement you bought, and the mention will help you connect with your target audience at the same time. All you have to do is come up with something worth writing about. Host an open house, for example, or sponsor a big sale and devote some of the proceeds to a local charity. Find a way to invest in your community and then alert the media to your good deeds… voila! Free publicity.

The point is your budget is more than just a dollar amount. You should be spending an equal amount of time working out how to allocate those funds so that you get the best return on your investment… regardless of how much or how little you have to spend.

And, as with everything else in the world of business, you need to have a system in place to track your results.

Google Analytics, for example, can tell you not only how many people are visiting your website, but also where they came from, what page(s) they viewed and which page was their last before they clicked away. This information can then tell you which pages are the most popular and which pages need more work. It will also reveal which referral sources are sending the most traffic your way… something that can help you decide which advertising venues work best for your business.

Having this kind of data gives you control over your marketing budget and thus, the campaign itself… and the more control you have in the area, the more effective you can be.

Lifetime Value of a Customer

Now, when considering how much you want to spend on marketing, you'll also want to take into account exactly what that money buys. After all, you're not really purchasing ad space or web hosting or printing services... what you're buying is access to your target market and if your marketing is effective, the dollars you spent for those efforts will be more than justified by the clients you bring into the fold.

Which brings us to the point of this section: just how much are your clients worth? Not just today, not just this month... but over the lifetime of their relationship with you.

Ironically, many business owners don't view clients in terms of long-term value—instead, they see a client's worth one sale at a time. But knowing the lifetime value can actually change the way you approach marketing, especially in terms of nurturing your herd and tending that lowest hanging fruit.

Now, the lifetime cycle will be different for each business sector and it's not just your marketing that will be affected. This number impacts your business model, your staffing, the skill sets required of your team and the management and leadership skills you'll need to thrive. Especially during turbulent times.

If, for example, you discovered that the average client offered a lifetime value of $75,000 over a 10-year period, you might not feel so bad about spending the extra $500 now for customer-loyalty programs. Likewise, that $75,000 makes it easier to justify paying a little more for the receptionist with the shining personality instead of just going with the cheapest candidate you can find.

Once you know the lifetime value of your customer, you can make more effective decisions. And calculating this number is relatively easy: Figure the average dollar amount per sale, per customer. Multiply that number by the average number of times a single client purchases within a year's time then multiply that number by the average number of years your clients will make those purchases—that is, the average lifetime you can expect to retain a given client.

The result is the average lifetime value your clients bring to your firm. Add to that the value that you can't measure—the glowing referrals your happy client gives to friends, family and colleagues for example—

and you're beginning to see just how much that client of yours is truly worth.

Client Acquisition Cost

In addition to knowing how much a customer is worth, you should also know how much it actually costs to acquire that customer. After all, if you're not spending enough, or worse, you're spending more than the lifetime value of the client, you're not really getting the benefit of your marketing efforts.

And if you're going to heed Dan Kennedy's advice—and you should—your goal should be to outspend your competitors to acquire a customer. But you can only do that with comfort and assurance when you know this metric.

Fortunately, this number is fairly easy to calculate as well: Simply divide the total cost of your marketing campaign for a given period by the number of new customers retained during that time.

One caveat: if your marketing campaign includes efforts to nurture existing clients—and it should—you'll have to factor that out if you want a true "new client acquisition" cost. If you've got a good reporting system in place, this should be relatively easy to do. If not, you'll have to estimate the nurture expense or, if nothing else, leave the numbers as they are and reconsider the need to upgrade how you track your numbers.

Revenue to Marketing Dollar Spent

Another big picture number I like knowing is how much revenue each campaign generates for each marketing dollar spent. I call it my marketing leverage ratio and it's a number that can give you great insight when deciding on marketing goals.

If I spend $1 on a campaign for example, I want to generate $8 in revenue. Your ratio, of course, will be specific to your profit goals and that's something you can determine through analysis. Understanding this ratio will also lead to a better analysis of other aspects of your business besides marketing—whether your closing methods are effective, for example, whether fulfillment is exceptional, whether service is truly top-notch and whether additional training is needed.

And as we've already seen, the more you know about your company and how it works, the more it can grow and prosper.

Some Final Thoughts on Marketing

I think the biggest mistake that I see, particularly in my profession—and probably in most professions—is that the business owner is expecting marketing success but expects somebody else to handle it. He or she has absolutely no understanding of it. So, they typically have a poor performing marketing system in place and really are not even aware of it.

I think the reason is two-fold. Number one: they don't educate themselves enough in that particular area; and, number two, they delegate the responsibility to somebody who comes in with a degree, title, past experience, or a resume that says they are marketers, without even knowing what to look for. They then have a false security because they have somebody in the marketing department. They think, "I've got that covered. So, let's get on with the business." The reality is there are very few people in the marketing industry in and of itself that even know what to do or how to do it.

— **Kelly Brown**, DDS
Owner, Custom Dental

When you talk about our unique selling proposition and our value statement—all that kind of stuff—we have for the last 20 years utilized the online web, worldwide web, company website, etc. As an organization, we get way too verbose. I am finding this great opportunity to relearn how to converse in an online text message, IM (instant message), Tweet, LinkedIn status update. I am relearning how to communicate with concise one-or-two-times-a-day important messages that are not perceived as junk or spam. I am really finding that it's completely changing the way I communicate when I actually have an opportunity to be verbose. It is a complete change of mindset.

My challenge for companies today is to learn how to use these tools. They are going to be important to the future. They will directly change your behavior and make you better at other things.

— Steve Harmon
Partner, Centriq Training

The starting point for the whole marketing perspective starts for me with, "Who is this company? Who are we? What is this company about?" I always go back to that discipline of market leaders that helps to figure out: which are your best products, lowest price or total solution. Then, that's where it starts. You must first identify who you are. I always start there, and then I move down to creating a competitive advantage. Who are you going to be after, and, how are you going to solve those people's problems.

— Sanford M. Fisch, JD
Co-Founder and CEO of the
American Academy of Estate Planning Attorneys

A lot of people think that effective delivery of the core product or service ought to entitle them to success. In reality that's supposed to be a given, but that's really just the admission ticket to the game and it ought not be looked at as any more than that.

In the current and evolving economy, people have more choices than ever before. They have more access to information about those choices than ever before. The pressure of commoditization and price suppression is greater than ever before. Literally, as we're having this conversation, one of the TV commercials being run for Apple's iPhone shows the price checking app. It shows a guy standing in one store about to buy something—some whiz bang coffee maker—and he pulls up the coffee maker on his iPhone. It tells him within a six block radius what stores sell it and what every store has it priced at in order of price affordability. He's happy as a clam because he can now walk six steps away and buy it for $4.00 less.

Consider this analogy for everything. They have more choices. They have more access to information. Commoditization is being driven by those factors and by this media of the internet. Coupled with that, now and for at least short-term foreseeable future, they either are trying to be more prudent as consumers; or, at least feel more prudent as consumers, because they've been economically beat-up by the recession. Put all that together?... Getting a customer and keeping a customer—just by being good enough or even being great at the core product or service—isn't going to cut it. That means going the extra mile. It means added value. It means a "wow" experience. It means creating reasons for someone to prefer you versus any and all others to such an extent that shopping, comparison shopping of any kind really, isn't an issue. If you're not really into that, then you're going to be vulnerable, very vulnerable, to all these adverse forces.

— **Dan Kennedy**
Author, Advisor, Consultant, Business Coach
& Editor of Six Business Newsletters

It's important to have an image—brand identity is real. You must draw a big playing field. If you are selling a commodity, you must develop a strong brand.

— **Dick Savage**
Retired, President, United Rotary Brush Corporation

PART V
PERFORMANCE
Choosing Your Path Wisely

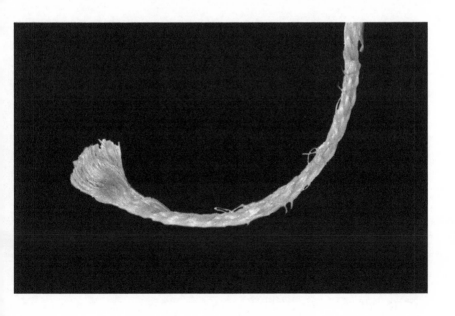

"Be a yardstick of quality. Some people aren't used to an environment where excellence is expected."

— Steve Jobs

WHEN THE PLAN FAILS

I know this book has given you a lot to think about as well as some invaluable tools that you can use to grow your business to amazing new heights. But no matter how inspired you might be or how many tools you might be carrying in your arsenal, that doesn't mean you won't still encounter some setbacks along the way. Turbulence will do that.

And it's important to address that now so that you'll be prepared to overcome them when they happen.

Setbacks come in all shapes and sizes. Even the best success stories are peppered with not-so-great moments... some of them downright devastating.

Apple co-founder, Steve Jobs, for example, was fired before putting it back on track to become the multi-billion dollar enterprise it is today. Harland Sanders—that's Colonel Sanders in case you didn't know—had his fried chicken recipe rejected over 1000 times before he finally got a restaurant to give it a try. Albert Einstein was expelled from school and labeled as mentally "slow" and anti-social. And Walt Disney was fired by a newspaper editor in his early years because, and I quote, "he lacked imagination and had no good ideas."

Yet, these people moved on to become some of the biggest movers and shakers in our history.

The question is how… how did they overcome those setbacks and go on to see such great success?

The truth is, overcoming obstacles and moving past setbacks isn't always easy. Sometimes it's just our pride that's been injured while other times it's our livelihood as we know it that's being threatened. And let's face it: it's not easy to think clearly when you're in a state of panic.

But thinking clearly is exactly what you should do and fortunately, there are a few ways to help you do just that:

Solicit Support

It's always important to surround yourself with a strong support network that includes friends and advisors, loved ones and colleagues. This support network can do everything from giving you kind words of encouragement to helping you draft out a new plan of action.

And what's great about having such a support network is that you'll find many have already experienced a similar situation. Having this kind of first-person experience helps you put things into perspective…. And perspective is a very important thing to have during a crisis.

Act Quickly

Remember those 12 tenets of successful business owners? Well, here's where at least one of those comes into play. When disaster strikes, you have to be ready to make hard decisions and make them fast. You don't want to act hastily of course, but you do want to have the presence of mind to do what needs to be done without second-guessing yourself.

Too often, business owners stick their head in the sand when faced with intimidating obstacles because they honestly believe that things will just "work themselves out." Sorry, but that rarely happens. In truth, things are likely to get worse. If you can't make payroll or can't fulfill orders, you need to make some decisions now about how you're going to handle that. And those decisions need to be rooted in the vision, mission, values and principles you laid out when you started this company.

Keep the Faith

If you look at all the hard-luck stories of famous entrepreneurs, you'll find one common ingredient that eventually led them to success: faith. They had faith in themselves and they had faith in their dream.

And it's easy to lose that faith when you're faced with dire circumstances, so you should figure out a way to remind yourself of your dream if that time ever comes. Remembering why you started this business, what it was you wanted to accomplish, what drove you to work all those hours and shoulder all that stress, will help you face down even the biggest obstacles and find a way around whatever it is that might be standing in your way.

Plan

If you weren't already convinced about the importance of planning, then hopefully you're rethinking the concept now. Having a plan means you know what to do when something goes terribly wrong. It means that you have alternate financing when the economy suddenly goes south and that you've already prepared for high gas prices, rolling blackouts or the sudden influx of competitors in your neighborhood.

Planning helps you maintain that perspective we were talking about and it also helps you take action because that action was conceived when you were in a better frame of mind. It gets you to thinking forward, not backward.

When discussing the importance of handling failure and dealing with setbacks, Tony Lewis weighed in with very useful insights.

"It's the responsibility of the leaders, the unit division, sales group or the CEO to recognize that things aren't going right, that we may have to retreat if strategies and plans are not working. We may have to retreat to fight the battle another day. Do it now and we will fight the battle another day. Delay and we may die."

The other side of that is that you should never think because you're the CEO or the commander that you're entitled to put people in a position where they follow you up the hill and go over the top without knowing what's on the other side. It has to be a crystallized plan. There has to be processes and then you have to give people enough latitude to make decisions on the fly.

In other words, if they know where you're going, if they know you're flying this airplane to San Francisco and that is the target, and you have a plan on how to get there and an alternate plan and shit happens— thunderstorms or the enemy—you still know where the target is and how you have to get there.

One last thought: There's always a solution; always an answer. You can be sure that you'll encounter at least a few obstacles on your path to success. Some will be easy to overcome... and some won't. The only constant here is that you'll always have control over how you choose to respond to those obstacles. That response may well be the deciding factor in your journey.

So, choose wisely, my friend... and allow the ripples of your decisions to propel you ever forward to conquer turbulent times and move you closer to your ultimate goals.

CONTINUOUS IMPROVEMENT: THE KEY TO PROSPERITY

You know what they say about the best laid plans… and in this case, *they* were right. It doesn't matter how much planning you do and how many preparations you make… the market will continue to change. Turbulence is a permanent element of our free enterprise system.

And you'll continue to be surprised.

So, if there's one final piece of advice that I can offer, it's this: Never stop improving, and innovating. In that quest, look for the big difference maker. The businesses that have survived difficult times did so because they were resilient. They recognized the changes in their industry or the economy or the preferences of their market, and they adapted to those changes without hesitation.

This ability to adapt also enabled them to look further down the road, and start leading their market instead of always reacting after the fact.

And this is the true mark of a leader.

You should be setting the pace, not struggling to keep up with it. You should be leading the pack… not trying to imitate what's already been done.

One of the things that made Steve Jobs and Apple so successful is the same mindset that enabled Henry Ford to design and build the famous

Model T automobile that revolutionized transportation: they both refused to follow the masses.

When asked about his Model T and the assembly line production system, Ford is quoted as saying, "If I asked the public what they wanted, they would say a faster horse." But, of course, Ford didn't give them what they wanted... he gave them what they needed.

And it's that same vision that enabled Steve Jobs to create innovative products that left his competition scrambling to duplicate.

This type of outside-the-box thinking is what will allow your company to thrive in turbulence when others falter. It's what will enable you to come up with "the next big thing" or know when to kill a product or service to lead your clients to something better.

That requires you to be on a constant mission of innovational improvement. Your job isn't to maintain the status quo nor is it to simply ride out the hard times in hopes of some economic relief ahead. You don't want things to stay the same because that means there isn't any room for you to grow. And consistent, controlled growth and profitability at each step along the way is the foundation of your prosperity.

These strategies will help you conquer turbulence. It will not be easy and there will be surprises. By definition turbulence brings the unexpected and in our reaction we reveal excellence or fissures in our business foundation. It's our reaction that governs our success against turbulence. This book has been about tools that empower us for an aggressive response to the unknown.

So, bring your best every day. Out work your opponents. Play hard. Go beyond the expected. Think. Think again. Don't quit. Win... turbulence be damned.

An Exclusive Offer from Larry Parman

Now that you've read the book, you're ready to take the next step. And if you're like most of the business owners I've known and worked with over the years, you're feeling pretty excited about the possibilities...

But, where do you go from here?

The truth is, there's no easy answer. How you proceed will depend greatly on a number of variables, including your industry, your market and of course, your vision. What you need, then, is a way to analyze your company from the ground up so that you can see exactly where you are, what you have to work with and what you still need to work on.

And let's be honest...some tips and resources on how to move forward wouldn't hurt either, right? Well, ask and you shall receive.

We've created a unique and comprehensive coaching program that will encompass all the different variables and philosophies we've introduced in this book. And as someone who has demonstrated a commitment to taking the next step toward success, I'd like to give you an exclusive sneak preview of this program... absolutely free!

To do that, we've created a new membership level that you can use to access some of our best tools and resources. Resources that include special reports on things like leadership, management and branding, plus worksheets and self-analysis tools you can use to start building your own Turbulence Thrival Plan.

Just go to http://CEOMaestro.com to sign up! There's no obligation and no cost to you... it's simply our way of helping entrepreneurs succeed during these turbulent times.

ABOUT THE CONTRIBUTORS

It is with humble appreciation that I acknowledge those that shared their time, advice, experiences and insights for this book. Some have been my mentors, others my colleagues or clients, all my friends. And each has touched my life in a significant way. This book would not be what it is without their generous contributions.

ED ALLEN

Ed Allen is a former U.S. Navy flag officer, a corporate executive and now leads an Executive Coaching and Consulting business. He specializes in coaching C level/equivalent executives to strengthen individual and team performance which impacts stronger bottom line results. He also specializes in coaching business professionals in transition.

Ed's first career was in the U.S. Navy and he achieved the rank of Rear Admiral. He led six operational commands: an F-14 Squadron, a Carrier Air Wing, an Amphibious Assault ship, an Attack Aircraft Carrier, Naval Space Command and a Carrier Battle Group/Commander NATO Strike Force. He served on the Navy Staff, the Joint Chiefs Staff and the Space/Naval Warfare Systems Command. Ed has a Master's Degree in International Affairs, graduated from the National War College, the Senior Officers Material

Readiness Course and completed Graduate Business studies in Information Technology. He was awarded the United States Navy League John Paul Jones Award for Inspirational Leadership and the Tailhooker of the Year Award. As a Naval Flight Officer, he accumulated over 3,300 flight hours, and 1285 arrested landings in 9 different types of aircraft.

As a Vice President of Business Development for the Oracle Corporation, Ed focused on e-Business solutions for Department of Defense Agencies, Navy/Marine Corps and Public Sector Health. He was also responsible for Oracle's Leadership and Executive Coaching initiative.

Ed's coaching clients include: Oracle, Northrop Grumman, Grant Thornton, Stanley Associates, Hawker Beechcraft Corp, Celanese Corp, CACI Corp, Alliance Systems, a former U.S. Senator, and Defense Department civilian and military leaders. He devotes a significant portion of his coaching practice to non-profit organizations.

He currently serves as Vice Chairman of the Board and Regional Director for Cherry Financial Partners, Inc. and as a Board Member of Xtreme Oil & Gas Corp.

ROBERT ARMSTRONG, JD

Co-founder of the American Academy of Estate Planning Attorneys, the California law firm, Armstrong, Fisch & Tutoli and Best Legal Practices, an internet marketing company designed to help attorneys embrace the digital revolution. A practicing attorney since 1976, Robert is a national speaker and co-author of several books, including *The E-Myth Attorney: Why Most Legal Practices Don't Work and What to Do About It* and *Dominate Your Market: The Attorney's Complete Guide to Online Marketing and Social Media*.

MICK ASLIN

Mick Aslin has served as the Chairman of Alterra Bank in Overland Park, Kansas since May, 2010.

He has been an influential part of the banking community in the Kansas City area for years, having previously served as President of Gold Bank in Overland Park and President of United Missouri Bank in Kansas City, Missouri.

BOB BARNARD

Bob is the President and Founder of Barnard Dunkelbert & Company, a nationally recognized airport planning firm with offices in Tulsa, Oklahoma and Denver, Colorado. Founded in 1976, Barnard Dunkelberg & Company is solely engaged in airport planning and environmental planning projects for civilian and military airports and associated communities. As its creative principal, Bob leads by example and has enabled Barnard Dunkelberg & Company to evolve as a leader in the industry.

BRYAN BEAVER

Bryan J. Beaver was introduced to the petroleum marketing industry in 1983 when he worked for a customer of Carter Petroleum (now CarterEnergy Corporation) and developed a mutual admiration with Sam K. Carter, the company's founder.

He went to work as the company's first marketing representative in 1983 and assumed the role of Sales Manager in 1987, vice President of Marketing in 1992 and then President in 1997.

Today, Bryan serves as the company's owner, CEO and President.

Bryan is very active with SIGMA, a non-profit, national trade association representing the most successful, progressive, and innovative independent motor fuel marketers and chain retailers in the U.S. He currently holds two Second Vice President appointments on both the Board and the executive Committee. He is also a Member of the ConocoPhillips Regional Council.

A lifelong resident of Kansas City, Bryan has been married to his wife Nancy for 30 years.

KELLY BROWN, DDS

Kelly Brown founded Custom Dental in 2011. Using proven practice management strategies and team building strategies, he has expanded his company to include 10 locations in two states. Custom Dental currently employs or partners with almost 100 Custom Dental contributors and provides over 350,000 dental services to their surrounding communities.

DENNIS M. CURTIN

President of RE/MAX Mid-States and Dixie Region, Dennis Curtin began his career as a real estate agent working for a small brokerage in North Kansas City, Missouri after graduating from Rockhurst College in 1972. He purchased his first RE/MAX franchise in 1975 and grew that single office venture to three offices housing over 110 associates and boasting a sales volume in excess of $200 million when he sold the company in 1990.

In June, 1993, he purchased the RE/MAX Dixie Region, including sub-franchise rights for Alabama, Louisiana and Mississippi, where he continues to serve as President. That region currently has 101 offices with over 1,400 associate members. He earned his Certified Real Estate Brokerage Manager designation in 1993, after completing the requirements in less than one year and he went on to earn the National Association of Realtors Certified International Property Specialists designation in 2000.

JOHN DUDECK

John Dudeck has a lengthy history of success in the real estate field. He currently serves as President of Guardian Equity Group in the San Francisco, CA area. Guardian collaborates with institutional investors throughout the country to acquire and manage a portfolio of income properties in the western United States. John has also served in a coaching capacity for many executives, including as an author.

A few years ago he wanted to create a series of success ideas he thought would be important for his son Jonathan as he entered the adult world. As the list grew, John and his wife, Diane, decided to make it a larger project. That notion resulted in them collaborating to write a book, *How to Get an "A" in Life*. John and Diane, a senior executive with Cisco, currently reside in Los Altos, CA.

CARL EDWARDS

Carl Edwards is a partner of Price Edwards & Company, the largest Oklahoma-based commercial real estate service company and of PEC Investment Properties, LLC, a related entity that has some ownership in real estate properties. He obtained his BA from the University of Oklahoma in 1970 and then went on to obtain his Masters in Business Administration from the University of Texas at Austin in 1972.

He is an active member of Oklahoma City's Commercial Real Estate Council, Chairman of the Board of Directors of Greater Oklahoma City Chamber of Commerce, Chairman of the Board of Trustees for Presbyterian Health Foundation and an Advisory Member of the Board of Trustees and Past President of the Board of Trustees for the Oklahoma Health Center Foundation. He is also the Chairman of the Oklahoma Bioscience Association and a member of the Board of Trustees and Chairman of the Oklahoma City Metropolitan Area Public Schools Trust.

SANFORD M. FISCH, JD

Sanford Fisch is co-founder and CEO of the American Academy of Estate Planning Attorneys, the total solution for estate planning and elder law firms nationwide. Since 1993 the Academy has provided its members with state-of-the-art law practice management tools and educational resources. By combining his keen business sense with an unparalleled understanding of law firm management, marketing and client relations, he has been instrumental in the growth of the Academy and the success of its programs. A practicing attorney since 1980, Sandy co-founded the law firm of Armstrong, Fisch & Tutoli and is a recognized leader and advisor to law firms throughout the United States.

BILL GLAZER

President of Bill Glazer Consulting and former owner and CEO of Glazer-Kennedy Insider's Circle, Bill Glazer is a much sought after public speaker, marketing consultant and distinguished copywriter. Known best for his "Outrageous Marketing" program, Bill has been featured in numerous marketing magazines around the world.

He won the RAC award at the 2002 Retail Advertising Conference (the advertising and marketing industry's equivalent to an Emmy or Oscar) and was also recruited by Dan Kennedy to partner with him to teach the masses their unique approach to direct response marketing.

MICHAEL J. GLOSSERMAN

Michael J. Glosserman is a Managing Partner and Chair of the Executive Committee of The JBG Companies. He began his career as a staff attorney with the U.S. Department of Justice, shortly thereafter moving into commercial real estate investment and development with the Rouse Company in 1972 and then joining JBG in 1979. He is a Board Member of the CoStar Group.

Non professional affiliations include: Chairman of the Board, National Building Museum; Executive Board Trustee, Federal City Council; and Advisory Board Member of the University of Pennsylvania Institute for Urban Research. He received his undergraduate degree from the Wharton School at the University of Pennsylvania and received his Juris Doctor from the University of Texas Law School.

STEVE HARMON

Raised by entrepreneurial parents where dinner table conversations ranged from payables to cash flow, the art, science and game of business is in Steve Harmon's blood.

Combining the passions of technology and business, he graduated from the University of Kansas which culminated in the incorporation of Executive Automation Consultants in 1987 and the addition of Network Institute of America in 1989. After renaming the two companies to US Connect in 1993, Steve sold the entity to IKON in 1996, launching what has continued to be a very successful entrepreneurial adventure.

He's currently a partner at Centriq Training, Kansas City's largest and most experienced IT training provider.

KIRK HUMPHREYS

Kirk Humphreys is chairman of The Humphreys Company, a real estate development firm that specializes in creating mixed-use communities.

Kirk served as Mayor of Oklahoma City from 1998 through 2003. He remains active in the community serving on the boards of OGE Energy Corp., the Oklahoma City Airport Trust and the Hough Ear Institute. Kirk also is co-host of Flash Point, a weekly televised commentary and debate on issues of local and national interest.

Kirk and Danna have been married for 39 years and have 3 children and 7 grandchildren.

GREG HUNT

Gregory L. Hunt, Ph.D. is a highly-regarded speaker, consultant, and writer and President of Directions, Inc. He leverages his wide-ranging work in the worlds of church, community, business, academia, counseling, and relationship education to help people think holistically and purposefully about their lives, relationships, and organizations.

In addition to his own involvements, he and his wife, Priscilla, are much in demand as a keynote speaking couple. They travel extensively, leading faith-based and non-sectarian couple conferences and retreats. They call metro Kansas City home. You can learn more about Greg's projects at www. GregoryLHunt.com.

STANLEY F. HUPFELD

Stanley Hupfeld became President and Chief Executive Officer of Oklahoma Healthcare Corporation and its subsidiaries in 1987. He then led the merger of Baptist Medical Center, Southwest Medical Center, and Baptist Healthcare of Oklahoma to form INTEGRIS Health, an integrated delivery system comprising 13 hospitals, in 1995. Twenty-three years later, he accepted the position of Chariman of the INTEGRIS Family of Foundations. Prior to his career with INTEGRIS Health, Mr. Hupfeld served as President of All Saints Healthcare in Fort Worth, Texas, for ten years. He served in the U.S. Army from 1968 to 1970.

A Texas native, he has an undergraduate degree in History from the University of Texas in Austin, and a Masters of Science in Healthcare Administration from Trinity University. He served as Campaign Chairman and Chairman of the Board of the United Way in both Fort Worth and Oklahoma City and continues to serve on the Board of Directors of the Oklahoma City Chamber of Commerce.

He has an extensive speaking background, and has been widely published, including the recent release of *Political Malpractice* on Amazon.com. He was honored in 2007 with one of the American Hospital Association's highest honors, The Award of Honor, and is also the recipient of the Friends of Nursing Award from the Oklahoma Nurses Association, the CEO Marketer of the Year award from the American Society for Healthcare Planning and Marketing and the Executive of the Year award from the Sales & Marketing Executives International. As the driving force of the nation's first hospital-sponsored charter school, he was recently honored in 2009 when the INTEGRIS Health Board of Directors voted to rename the school The Stanley Hupfeld Academy at Western Village. He currently writes a healthcare column for a local business daily, the *Journal Record*.

DAN KENNEDY

Perhaps one of the best-known and successful entrepreneurs, Dan Kennedy is an accomplished author of multiple books and renowned direct-response marketing consultant. Through his newsletters, tele-coaching programs, local Chapters and study groups, he has influenced millions of independent business owners around the world.

Dan is a well-known public speaker and has appeared with four former U.S. Presidents, business celebrities, entrepreneurs and famous coaching and business experts such as Zig Ziglar and Tony Robbins.

His books are available at Amazon.com, BN.com and bookstores. Free information can be obtained at www.NoBSBooks.com.

TONY LEWIS

Tony Lewis is a 37- year experienced business executive with a proven management ability to lead the strategic, capital, technical, and human resource disciplines of diverse domestic and international organizations. He started his business career in 1974 with Continental Grain Company and was involved in this country's first major grain sale to the Russians. From there, he joined Con Agra as its President, where he engineered a major new strategic direction for the company, which led to years of predictable and consistent performance. He attributed many of his successes to what he learned in his second career as a 39 year Command Pilot, Instructor and Operations Commander in the Air Force and Air Force Reserves. The lessons learned from war and how those same principles of leadership and disciplines apply to business is a favorite topic that he often speaks about to CEO's and management teams.

Since 1997, Mr. Lewis has been Chairman of 3 working advisory groups of CEO's who meet once a month in a safe and confidential venue to help them make better decisions and more timely decisions relative to increasing the effectiveness and enhancing the lives of their organizations. The name of the venue is "Vistage".

Mr. Lewis is 65 years old. He has a degree in Agricultural Economics. He has served on many boards of directors during his business career and has held seats on the Chicago Board of Trade, Minneapolis Board of Trade and the Kansas City Board of Trade. In the past 5 years he has served on the public company board of directors of Torotel Inc. and is a member of the audit committee and Chairman of the compensation committee. He has been married for 39 years with 2 grown children.

AVIS PARMAN
Avis Parman retired as an active bank executive in 1998 and continues living in Northwest Missouri. She has been the recipient of numerous professional, civic and leadership awards during her career.

She rang the closing bell at the New York Stock Exchange in 2003 as Vice President and board member of the Business and Professional Women's National Foundation.

DICK SAVAGE
After a ten-year stint with Standard Oil Company, Richard E. Savage decided to start his own commercial real estate development and property management business in 1975. In 1983 –after a severe downturn in the real estate industry—he turned his focus to a small runway rotary brush manufacturing business in Lenexa, Kansas. Over the next two decades, he grew the company from $900,000 in revenue to $35,000,000 and became the dominate manufacturer in that industry. He sold the company to Westshore Capital Partners in 2008.

Dick has been married for 47 years and continues to enjoy his retirement by assisting his wife in her day care business and serving on the Foundation Board of Trustees for the University of Northern Iowa. He and his wife call Palm Desert, California, home and enjoy their role as grandparents to their three grandsons.

DICK SEYBOLT
Friend, satisfied client, fellow Vistage member and one glad to contribute to the success of others. Dick is the CEO of Diamond Coach Corp.

LINDA WINLOCK
Linda Winlock is the owner and President of Personnel Profiling Inc. Established in 1987, Personnel Profiling provides organization development,

employment assessments and human resource services to companies throughout the nation. She has over 20 years of experience working with all types of industries and company sizes. Her formal education includes a Master's Degree in Education with a concentration in counseling psychology.

In addition, Linda is a Strategic Business Partner and Area Director for Profiles International. Profiles International is an industry leader in employment assessments and provides services to over 40,000 clients in 122 countries.

About Larry Parman

His clients will tell you Larry Parman offers a unique set of experience and skills to his executive coaching clients. Many say it's like having a one man board of directors, a trusted adviser who shares a wealth of legal, financial and high performance strategies that help companies grow and their owners improve bottom line results.

Mr. Parman's companies offer comprehensive legal, tax and financial services.

He is an attorney and the owner of Parman & Easterday, a law firm that concentrates in business, estate and tax planning services. He holds the Accredited Estate Planner designation from the National Association of Estate Planners and Counsels. Mr. Parman is the co-author of two books written for the consumer titled *Estate Planning Basics: A Crash Course in Safeguarding Your Legacy* and *Guiding Those Left Behind: What You Need to Know to Settle Your Estate.*

In addition, he is a licensed Series 7 FINRA registered representative, a Registered Investment Advisor and a partner in a firm offering its clients a full range of investment, retirement and insurance services and products. He was a contributing author of *Stop & Think: Important Financial Advice for You and Your Family*, a book covering various topics for the serious investor.

Early in his life Mr. Parman found himself wanting to know what motivated people, what those who were successful did that others did not. He became a serious student of leadership strategies that created transformational results. That journey continued from college days at the University of Missouri, where he was tapped as one of seven Outstanding University Seniors, into his military experience, where he was offered an opportunity to work on a task force updating the U.S. Army's Leadership Manual. Later on he became certified to instruct four programs for the Dale Carnegie organization as an avocational instructor—the Human Relations course; the Sales course; the Management Seminar; and the Strategic Presentations Workshop.

That work was the genesis for his partnership in Notch It Up Strategies, LLC, an online and offline marketing company, and CEO Maestro, a firm offering high impact coaching programs for C-level executives and business owners.

Mr. Parman is the author of *Above the Fray: Leading Yourself, Your Business and Others During Turbulent Times*. It is a resource every busy executive and business owner responsible for bottom line results must have in their reference library. In February, 2013, Governor Mary Fallin named Mr. Parman to her cabinet as Oklahoma's Secretary of State. In October, 2013, Governor Fallin named him as Oklahoma's Secretary of Commerce.

You may find more information about Larry Parman's coaching programs, workshop schedules, speaking engagements, and other resources to improve individual and organizational performance at www.CEOmaestro.com.